At Issue

Are Athletes
Good Role Models?

Other Books in the At Issue Series:

Age of Consent

Animal Experimentation

Are Adoption Policies Fair?

Beauty Pageants

Biofuels

Cancer

Cyberpredators

Drones

Fracking

Gay Marriage

High School Dropouts

Negative Campaigning

Reality TV

Tasers

Teen Smoking

What Is the Impact of Twitter?

At Issue

| Are Athletes
| Good Role Models?

Thomas Riggs & Company, Book Editor

GREENHAVEN PRESS
A part of Gale, Cengage Learning

Farmington Hills, Mich • San Francisco • New York • Waterville, Maine
Meriden, Conn • Mason, Ohio • Chicago

Elizabeth Des Chenes, *Director, Content Strategy*
Cynthia Sanner, *Publisher*
Douglas Dentino, *Manager, New Product*

For more information, contact:
Greenhaven Press
27500 Drake Rd.
Farmington Hills, MI 48331-3535
Or you can visit our Internet site at gale.cengage.com

Articles in Greenhaven Press anthologies are often edited for length to meet page requirements. In addition, original titles of these works are changed to clearly present the main thesis and to explicitly indicate the author's opinion. Every effort is made to ensure that Greenhaven Press accurately reflects the original intent of the authors. Every effort has been made to trace the owners of copyrighted material.

Cover image © GStar.

LIBRARY OF CONGRESS CATALOGING-IN-PUBLICATION DATA

Are athletes good role models? / Thomas Riggs & Company, book editor.
    p. cm. -- (At issue)
    Summary: "At Issue: Are Athletes Good Role Models?: Books in this anthology series focus a wide range of viewpoints onto a single controversial issue, providing in-depth discussions by leading advocates, a quick grounding in the issues, and a challenge to critical thinking skills"-- Provided by publisher.
    Includes bibliographical references and index.
    ISBN 978-0-7377-6820-6 (hardback) -- ISBN 978-0-7377-6821-3 (paperback)
    1. Athletes--Conduct of life--Juvenile literature. 2. Role models--Juvenile literature. I. Riggs, Thomas, 1963-
    GV706.8.A76 2014
    306.4'83--dc23
                               2013038428

796
A

Printed in the United States of America
1 2 3 4 5 6 7 18 17 16 15 14

Contents

Introduction   7

1. Athletes Are in a Unique Position   11
   to Influence Society
   Leigh Steinberg

2. It's Unfair to Expect Athletes to Serve   16
   as Role Models
   Lane Wallace

3. Seeing Through the Illusions   23
   of the Sports Hero
   William C. Rhoden

4. African American Athletes Have a Right   29
   and a Duty to Be Role Models
   Mike Tillery

5. Female Athletes Empower Young Women   34
   Despite Objectification
   Joe Posnanski

6. Athletes Can Be Leaders in Ending   40
   Homophobia
   Brendon Ayanbadejo

7. Christian Athletes Set an Example of Humility   44
   Bryan Cribb

8. Christian Athletes Are Not Role Models   49
   Mark Galli

9. Paralympians Are Inspirations for All   55
   *James Mastro, Christopher Ahrens, and Nathan
   Statton*

10. Marketers Need Stricter Moral Clauses   **61**
to Police Athlete Behavior
Christopher R. Chase

11. Love Versus Hate: How Fans Cope   **65**
with Athletes' Transgressions
Leeja Carter

12. Lessons Can Be Learned from   **70**
Athletes' Mistakes
Steve Tobak

13. Sports Scandals Reflect the Culture at Large   **75**
Dennis Maley

Organizations to Contact   **82**
Bibliography   **87**
Index   **92**

Introduction

Human beings have long looked toward athletes for inspiration. The ancient Greeks staged the first Olympic Games in the year 776 BC, competing in foot and chariot races, wrestling matches, and field events such as discus and javelin throws to honor Zeus, the father of the gods. Athletes travelled from as far as Spain to compete in the games, and the winners of each event were crowned with olive wreaths and heralded publically for bringing honor upon their city, their family, and themselves. Often the winners would be commemorated via *epinikia*—victory songs composed by poets exalting the athlete as a paragon of strength and virtue—or larger-than-life statues and monuments meant to display the champion's superiority. Some ancient Greek historians went so far as to liken Olympic champions to mythological heroes—mortals, often descended from the gods, whose legendary feats of strength and endurance were retold throughout the generations to motivate and instruct young men and women in the meaning of courage, perseverance, and self-confidence.

Our infatuation with the athletic spectacle continues unabated to this day. Major sporting events such as the modern Olympics, World Cup, Super Bowl, World Series, Stanley Cup playoffs, and the National Collegiate Athletic Association (NCAA) College Basketball Tournament are among the most highly watched and attended sporting contests in the world. A 2011 study by management consulting firm A.T. Kearny found the global sports industry to be worth between \$480 billion and \$620 billion. A significant portion of that total can be attributed to today's olive wreath, the multimillion dollar endorsement deal that is all but guaranteed to the top athletes in every sport. Another portion comes from the sale of sports paraphernalia and memorabilia, such as authentic jerseys bearing star athletes' names, which allow fans to not only show their support for their favorite teams but to imagine that they themselves are the ones scoring the game-winning goal, catching the fifty-yard pass, or pitching the perfect game.

Modern sports stars occupy such a prominent place in our cultural imagination that they are often credited with single-handedly altering the course of history: baseball player Jackie Robinson broke the color barrier in professional sports by becoming the first African American athlete to play major league baseball in 1947, paving the way for the civil rights movement of the 1960s; female tennis player Billie Jean King legitimized women's sports and bolstered the feminist movement by beating male tennis champion Bobby Riggs in the 1973 "Battle of the Sexes"; the 1980 US men's Olympic ice hockey team gave the United States a crucial psychological edge in the Cold War by defeating the heavily favored Soviet Union team in the "Miracle on Ice." Other powerful moments of individual athletic accomplishment—one-handed pitcher Jim Abbott throwing a no-hitter in 1993; Kerri Strug enduring the pain of torn ankle tendons and landing a perfect vault to lead the US women's gymnastics team to their first Olympic gold team medal in 1996; Michael Jordan fighting through the stomach flu (later revealed to be food poisoning) to score thirty-eight points in a pivotal NBA (National Basketball Association) playoff game in 1998—stand as contemporary hero myths, cultural touchstones that inspire us to persevere when faced with obstacles of our own.

But with such adulation also comes increased scrutiny. In 1993, outspoken NBA star Charles Barkley decried the increased attention that was being paid to his and other athletes' off-court antics in a television commercial, stating, "I am not a role model. I'm not paid to be a role model. I am paid to wreak havoc on the basketball court. Parents should be role models." Fellow basketball star Karl Malone responded to the ad with a column in *Sports Illustrated* arguing that, "We don't choose to be role models, we are chosen. Our only choice is whether to be a good role model or a bad one." In today's age of the 24/7 news media, cell phone cameras, and social networking sites that allow an individual to snap a photo or a video clip and share it with the world in a matter of seconds, athletes are even more a part of the public eye, and the debate over their rights and responsibilities has intensified.

Some commentators argue that athletes are too driven by greed, ego, and an unhealthy desire to win at all costs to serve as positive examples for the rest of society, particularly when these traits reveal themselves off the court or playing field. Many point to a series of recent scandals related to sports stars as evidence: Pittsburgh Steelers quarterback Ben Roethlisberger and Los Angeles Lakers guard Kobe Bryant were accused of sexual assaults in 2010 and 2003, respectively. Seven-time Tour de France winner Lance Armstrong was stripped of his titles in 2013 when he admitted to using banned substances in order to get an edge on his opponents, joining baseball players Mark McGwire, Barry Bonds, Sammy Sosa, and Roger Clemens, Olympic sprinter Marion Jones, and several other top-level athletes who have either admitted to or have been strongly suspected of using performance enhancing drugs (PEDs). Superstar golfer Tiger Woods' chronic marital infidelities became tabloid fodder in 2009. And Atlanta Falcons quarterback Michael Vick was convicted in 2007 of running an illegal dogfighting ring from his home and spent nineteen months in prison. The list goes on and on, and in almost every case these athletes lost millions of dollars in endorsement contracts while being labeled as villains in the eyes of the once-adoring public.

Others, however, suggest that despite their propensity for letting down fans, athletes do a great deal of good for society. Beyond inspiring us to reach for ever-greater heights of personal accomplishment, they teach fans—particularly young fans—important lessons in cooperation, hard work, sportsmanship, even graciousness in defeat. Many athletes come from disadvantaged communities, and their success can motivate youths from similar backgrounds to direct their energy toward healthy activities rather than criminal ones. Moreover, these athletes often give back to their communities by establishing charities, funding the construction of new courts and playing fields, and volunteering their time at sports camps or other public events. Courageous athletes are still challenging social boundaries and giving hope to entire segments of society that were previously shunned in the sports world: female auto racer Danica Patrick has risen to prominence in a traditionally male-dominated sport, and NBA player Jason Collins became the first male athlete in major professional team sports to come out as gay in April of 2013. Even those athletes who let us down can be credited with teaching us valuable lessons in what *not* to do.

As the variety of viewpoints in this volume show, the debate over athletes' ability to serve as role models often goes beyond questioning the place of sports in society, taking on religious and philosophical dimensions that challenge our perceptions of human nature and the athlete-fan relationship. While it is quite clear that no one, from sports stars to religious and political leaders to business moguls, can be counted on to always live up to the high standards and ideals that we set for them, it is equally clear that there is an innate need in society to hold these figures up as examples of the best that humanity has to offer. Because of sports' ability to elevate a relatively unknown figure to international superstardom as the result of a single play, there are unlimited opportunities for today's young athletes to become the next generation of sports role models. Yet, given the ability of the sports media and fans alike to scrutinize every moment in an athlete's life, there are an equal number of opportunities for today's role models to become tomorrow's fallen stars.

1

Athletes Are in a Unique Position to Influence Society

Leigh Steinberg

Leigh Steinberg is a sports agent and athlete advocate who has represented top athletes in every major sport. He coauthored the best-selling book Winning with Integrity: Getting What You Want Without Selling Your Soul *(1999) and is a regular public speaker on sports and athlete-related issues.*

Athletes can and should serve as role models to society. Sports stars are in a unique position to use their wealth and influence to support disaffected communities (from which many star athletes themselves came) and to offer a positive example to young fans who lack strong parental guidance.

It was an ugly week in the world of sports. Lance Armstrong, the all-American cancer survivor who set the record in cycling for most Tour De France championships admitted to Oprah [Winfrey, celebrity host] that he achieved his victories by doping. [College football player] Manti Te'o, a nationwide icon for the courage he displayed in playing on the same day he learned about the death of his grandmother and girlfriend, revealed that his girlfriend was a hoax. [Football player] Andre Smith of the [Cincinnati] Bengals was detained at an airport for trying to take a concealed weapon on a plane. Fallout continues from the autopsy report demonstrating that [professional football player] Junior Seau suffered from multiple concussions leading to chronic traumatic encephalopathy—which leads to depression and potential suicide. The sports page reads much more like the crime beat or business section of a newspaper due to the drumbeat of off-field problems. This all raises the question as to whether it is appropriate to look to athletic figures as role models and whether they should be held up to circumspect levels of conduct. With the constant chronicling of every athletic misbehavior, are athletes the right symbols?

My friend, former NBA [National Basketball Association] superstar and current television analyst Charles Barkley is clear that the answer is a resounding "NO!" He believes that athletes are not the figures that children should be emulating. He feels that it is parents who have the obligation and responsibility to be role models. He believes players have a duty to give peak performance on the court, and that is it. I have built a 40-year career in representation around the belief that athletes are role models and can trigger imitative behavior. Who is right?

Information is delivered to the public in a greatly enhanced and expanded way in this era—multiple platforms providing 24-hour content. The celebrity making machine with its focus on interesting personalities brings celebrities into our living rooms daily. Satellite television means exponentially more games broadcast, more analysis, more focus on personality than previously imagined. That television monitor acts as a magnifying glass, which produces athletic performance and personality in larger than life detail. It is inescapable. Athletes will be figures of admiration and emulation in this sports obsessed society. Parents have a critical role to play in shaping their children's values and behavior. The unfortunate truth is that many families have absent parents or individuals incapable of providing sound guidance. Young people will look to athletes whether we wish them to or not.

Athletes that still play at a competitive level after high school are really participants in the entertainment business. Collegiate players may not be paid but they and their professional brethren play for colleges or professional organizations that are dependent on public support. Sports are not food on the table or shelter or transportation—all critical needs for survival. It is a discretionary entertainment business competing for fan viewership, ticket sales, and other revenue streams with other sports, movies, HBO [cable television], video games, outdoor recreation, Walt Disney World and every other form of entertainment. If fans become disillusioned by athletic behavior—force-fed negative incidents or too many contract squabbles or destructive CBA [collective bargaining agreement] deadlocks—they can easily turn their attention elsewhere. A professional player who doesn't want to sign autographs, graciously grant press interviews, or comport themselves publicly within acceptable norms of behavior has an alternative—he can play on a sandlot. No one will criticize, judge or have any expectations. They also will not be paid huge sums for playing or endorsements or have any of the fame or exalted lifestyle that ensues.

Disaffected teenagers may tune out authority figures— parents, teachers, and commercial messages. A superstar athlete can permeate that perceptual screen to deliver a message of inspiration and hope.

Athletes Give Back

I have asked athletes to envision themselves as role models and responsible members of the communities that helped build and shape them. This does not assume they will at every moment be behaviorally correct, we all make mistakes and mature and grow from them. But over 120 of our clients established scholarship funds or retrofitted athletic equipment or helped their church or Boy's and Girl's Club at the community they grow up in. They retrace their roots. A number of players like [football player] Troy Aikman and [baseball player] Eric Karros at UCLA [University of California Los Angeles], [football players] Edgerrin James at [University] of Miami, Kerry Collins at Penn State, have endowed scholarships at their colleges—setting an example for younger players and staying linked to that college community. At the professional level, we asked that athletes find a cause near to them to have a foundation that could help. They enlisted leading business, political and community leaders to assist. Years ago, San Diego [Chargers] place kicker [Rolf Benirschke] started "Kicks For Critters" to raise funds and awareness for endangered species research at the San Diego Zoo. It had a poster/pledge card component, which was the genesis for many later donations for individual achievement programs. Derrick Thomas, [Kansas City] Chiefs linebacker, remedied childhood reading problems with his "Third and Long" program in Kansas City. [Football player] Steve Young has a "Forever Young Foundation" to aid children's charities in the San Francisco Bay Area. [Football player] Warren Moon's Crescent Moon Foundation operated in Houston, Minneapolis, Seattle and Southern California to fund college scholarships for needy high school students.

What all these athletes were modeling was their heart, initiative and the ability for all of us to improve our communities and tackle problems. They are not modeling the chance for millions of young people to be professional athletes—that is only a gateway for the few. But when Heavyweight Boxing Champion Lennox Lewis said on a public service announcement that "Real Men Don't Hit Women" he made a great contribution to young people's perception of what is embodied in true masculinity. Disaffected teenagers may tune out authority figures—parents, teachers, and commercial messages. A superstar athlete can permeate that perceptual screen to deliver a message of inspiration and hope.

This country needs role models and athletes have both an incredible opportunity and responsibility to use their power for good.

2

It's Unfair to Expect Athletes to Serve as Role Models

Lane Wallace

Lane Wallace is a former pilot and prominent aviation writer who has written several books on aviation, athletic endurance, and adventure seeking, including Unforgettable: My 10 Best Flights *(2009) and* Surviving Uncertainty: Taking a Hero's Journey *(2009).*

The tragic story of Oscar Pistorius—the South African double amputee who competed in the 2012 Olympics using prosthetic legs—having been arrested for the murder of his girlfriend in February 2013 highlights the fact that our most successful and idolized athletes are often deeply flawed individuals. For many star athletes, their competitive drive and oversized ego inhibit their ability to participate in mainstream society, making it impossible for them to live up to the idealized standards we hold for role models and heroes.

The news from the South African capital of Pretoria last Thursday [February 14, 2013] came as a disappointment of the highest, most crushing nature. We'd had athletes plummet to notoriety dramatically and recently, but not like this. The fall of cancer survivor-turned-Tour-de-France-champion Lance Armstrong, for example, at least offered the mercy of a gradual unveiling. By the time Armstrong himself came clean, it was almost like physically losing a father after years of Alzheimer's deterioration had already taken away the important parts.

But the news that Oscar Pistorius, the South African who became the first double amputee to compete against able-bodied runners at the London Olympics last summer [2012], had been arrested for the murder of his supermodel girlfriend on Valentine's Day, was more brutally shocking, on several levels.

First, and most obviously, the crime of doping pales dramatically compared with murder. Second, there were no highly publicized rumors of [heavyweight boxer] Mike-Tyson-type bad behavior leading up to the incident, so we (the general fan/reader public) had no warning. Our image adjustment was abrupt and severe. And third, the news shattered a fantasy story—or stories—that we really, really wanted to believe.

The obvious fantasy personified by Pistorius is of the underdog overcoming overwhelming adversity to achieve triumph. A man without legs reaches the semi-finals of the 400-meter track event at the Olympics? "If that can happen," one can just hear parents around the world telling their children, "then you can do anything." Even if you're not perfect. Or you have some physical defect. Or you're sick.

It's a powerful and uplifting message that we want to believe, in all its simplicity and potential for a happy ending. Fade to credits, everyone leaves inspired.

Unfortunately, the equation of achievement is far more complex.

Champions Never Rest

In a revealing profile of [basketball star] Michael Jordan at 50, published this week [February 17, 2013] on ESPN.com, Wright Thompson writes that the young Jordan believed his father preferred his older brother, and spent a lifetime driven to achieve as a way of proving his worth. "This appetite to prove—to attack and to dominate and to win," Thompson notes, ". . . has been successful and spectacularly unhealthy."

Even Jordan acknowledged that his self-esteem has always been "tied directly to the game." Hence the drive, the rage, the relentless pursuit of victory that led to astounding feats of skill and six championship rings in his dresser drawer. But Jordan also talked to Thompson about what the process of that pursuit does to a person. "You ask for these special powers to achieve these heights, and now you got it and you want to give it back, but you can't. . . . I drove myself so much that I'm still living with some of those drives. . . . I don't know how to get rid of it."

It's an aspect to achievement that we often shove aside in our focus on the shining moments of record-breaking triumph. And that goes for more than just sporting feats and icons. A friend of mine, whose job gave him access to many of the top CEOs in America, told a similar tale about their motivations and demons. I'd kidded him, back in my single days, to keep me in mind if he knew an interesting CEO who was single and age-appropriate.

"I do," he answered. "But the truth is, I wouldn't wish any of them on you."

"Why?" I asked.

To be a Michael Jordan or a gold-medal Olympic athlete requires such single-minded focus that it also necessarily requires trading off a whole lot of balance in life and development.

"Because they're generally not easy on their wives or families," he answered. He went on to explain that he'd developed a theory about top-achieving CEOs [chief executive officers]. "Almost to a person, they've been denied something that really mattered to them, early in their lives. So they spend the rest of their lives making up for it. Achieving. And not only does that make them pretty focused on themselves, it also means that no achievement is ever enough. They're driven."

That, mind you, is before you throw in the ego that develops with success or the impact that sudden wealth, power, and fame can have on people who are ill-prepared to cope with it. You spend years laser-focused on yourself and your own achievement. And then, if you're successful, suddenly everyone else is focused on you, as well. As Thompson noted, "[Jordan] is used to being the most important person in every room he enters and, going a step further, in the lives of everyone he meets." Those in Jordan's life, Thompson says, are well versed in not only his achievements, but also "his ego, his moods, and his anger."

Top-level achievement requires talent, to be sure. But it also requires tremendous focus and great sacrifice. It makes sense that many of the people willing to devote that kind of effort and make those sacrifices have some driving emotional or psychological need that makes the trade-offs worthwhile. For everything in life is most assuredly a trade-off. To be a Michael Jordan or a gold-medal Olympic athlete requires such single-minded focus that it also necessarily requires trading off a whole lot of balance in life and development—a weakness that can then be amplified with the rush of fame, money, and attention that success brings. Perhaps the surprising thing is that there are actually exceptions to the rule; top athletes, celebrities and CEOs who *do* manage to be balanced individuals, with balanced lives and an ability to focus on others instead of themselves.

An Excruciating Drive

In view of all that, it's not hard to believe that a kid who had both legs amputated at age one, who was six when his parents divorced and 15 when his mom died, would possess an excruciating drive to prove or overcome the insecurities or damage from those losses. Or that the same drive and traits that got him to the Olympics might be less suited for healthy interpersonal interactions. Or that the insecurities still lurked inside— demons that only got scarier with all the world's focus on him as a perfect poster child.

So maybe we shouldn't be so shocked. But we are. Because we don't want to look at the complexity or costs of achievement. We want to paint our heroes pure, so we can indulge in our happy-fantasy hero-worship without having to feel queasy about it.

It wasn't always so. The epic journey tales—from *The Odyssey* to the Arthurian and Holy Grail legends to *Star Wars*— always told of heroes who were flawed, and whose wisdom, strength, and triumph sometimes came at a messy cost and with many scars. We too often forget that fact in our modern equation of achievement with romantic appeal. It's a bit ironic, actually. Would Oscar Pistorius have had a cover girl model girlfriend like Reeva Steenkamp if he hadn't been an Olympic celebrity? Possibly not. Many women find competence attractive. The higher the achievement, and the more lauded a man's achievements are, the more appealing he will be to a whole lot of women, regardless of his other traits. And yet, the same traits that make those men celebrity athletes or super-achievers may, in fact, make them a bad bet as an actual romantic partner.

Granted, Pistorius would appear to be an extreme case. To be clear: All charges against Pistorius are alleged, at the moment. And domestic violence, if that proves to be the cause of Steenkamp's death, cuts across all segments of society, in the U.S. as well as abroad. High achievers do not have a corner on that market. The combination of insecurity, anger, and other damaged psychological traits that lead a person to abuse or turn violent toward women exists in all too many individuals and all too many places.

But it's worth pondering for a moment: For all of Michael Jordan's ego and anger and moods, two sportscasters discussing the ESPN piece last week noted that Jordan wasn't even in the top 50 of arrogant, egotistical sports figures they'd interviewed. That should give us pause, just as my friend's comments about the motivators and costs of top achievement in the business world gave me pause. Why do we view people who achieve great personal success or achievements—especially those that involve an almost narcissistic focus on themselves—as romantic figures or role models?

To admire our sports superstars while acknowledging the likelihood of the flaws that either contributed to their success or came about because of what that success required or created would take a lot of the fun out of our fantasies about them.

Nobody Has It All

We should, by all means, acknowledge great achievement. Because it *does* come at great cost. Nobody has it all. Nobody can have a level-10 career and excel in their personal life, as well. Not even men. They may *look* like they have it all, but they don't. Just ask their neglected wives and children. There are hard, firm trade-offs in where a person's time and energy get directed, and every choice has a consequence. (And there's much, much more that can and needs to be said on that subject.)

But when we look for role models, why do we gloss over all the demons, flaws, and costs, and build these singular high achievers into all-around "10s" in our images and minds? I'm not sure, but I suspect it's because we want to believe the fairy tale. We want to believe that Prince Charming actually *is* a great guy, through and through. We want the simple, happy ending. And, perhaps we also want to believe that we, too, can focus on ourselves and achieve whatever we want without someone else bearing the cost that achievement requires.

To admire our sports superstars while acknowledging the likelihood of the flaws that either contributed to their success or came about because of what that success required or created would take a lot of the fun out of our fantasies about them, of course. It might also make those athletes a little tougher to market. On the other hand, it might take a little pressure off of them and, as Michael Jordan put it, allow them to "breathe."

I recognize that there are far too many forces at play for that scenario to come about anytime soon, if ever. But imagine how the world might change if balance ever became as valued as singular achievement. Now, there's a fantasy I could get excited about.

3

Seeing Through the Illusions of the Sports Hero

William C. Rhoden

William C. Rhoden is a longtime sports columnist with The New York Times. *He has also written for the* Baltimore Sun *and served as associate editor for* Ebony *magazine. He has written two books on the African American athlete experience:* Forty Million Dollar Slaves: The Rise, Fall, and Redemption of the Black Athlete *(2007) and* Third and a Mile: The Trials and Triumphs of the Black Quarterback, an Oral History *(2007).*

Star athletes are not heroes. The concept of heroism, as it is commonly used to describe sports stars, is a myth that ignores human fallibility and sets up athletes for scandal and rejection, or otherwise forces fans and the media to overlook athletes' failures in order to perpetuate the myth. Instead, we must understand that, while top athletes may do amazing things on the field, they are not always good people off it.

That wise basketball philosopher Charles Barkley once declared, "I am not a role model."

A star with the Phoenix Suns at the time, Barkley was lambasted by a large portion of the news media who insisted that high-profile athletes, by virtue of their celebrity, should act like paragons of virtue, even if they weren't.

Barkley, in his text for a Nike advertisement, was referring to role models, not sports heroes, but the concepts come from the same deep-seated need to make things what they are not. We crave illusion, and athletes have historically been vessels of our self-deception. In light of the dramatic falls of [football player] Michael Vick, [track and field athlete] Marion Jones, [baseball players] Barry Bonds, Roger Clemens, [professional golfer] Tiger Woods and now [cyclist] Lance Armstrong, we need to either recalibrate our definition of the sports hero or scrap it altogether. The concept is based largely on ignorance: the less we know about an athlete, the easier it becomes to invest him with lofty ideals. The ideals have little to do with the athlete's character and everything to do with creating an artificial construct that serves a need.

Sports heroism contains a number of elements.

The Emotion of Heroism

There is the emotion of heroism.

My father loved Joe Louis [boxer] and Jesse Owens [track and field athlete], and he wasn't alone. They were icons of an era. After Louis defeated Primo Carnera in 1935, a writer for *The Los Angeles Times* gushed: "The colored race couldn't have chosen two more remarkable men than Jesse Owens and Joe Louis to be its outstanding representatives. Owens is being hailed as the greatest track and field athlete of all time, same thing goes for 'Dead Pan' Joe Louis, whose decisive defeat of Carnera has sent the scribes scurrying to the dictionaries seeking superlatives of greater scope than any they've used before."

The heroic reality, based on a myth to begin with, is often grim.

There is the propaganda of heroism.

Louis and Owens—the grandsons of slaves and the sons of sharecroppers—were tools of an American image-making machine designed to show the world, and Nazi Germany in particular, that the United States had it right.

But the heroic reality, based on a myth to begin with, is often grim.

Louis battled drug addiction for years, was forced to fight past his prime and wound up destitute. He appeared on TV game shows at the end of his career, wrestled professionally and spent time in a psychiatric institution.

When Owens refused to continue a tour across Europe after the 1936 Berlin Olympics, he was barred for life as a "professional" by the Amateur Athletic Union. He was hounded by the Internal Revenue Service and was even tracked by the F.B.I. [US Federal Bureau of Investigation], which monitored his talks abroad to make sure Owens was no Paul Robeson [African American singer and actor active in the Civil Rights Movement].

As Owens headed to the ballpark one afternoon to participate in yet another cheesy moneymaking exhibition, he came across an article in that day's *New York Post* that poignantly described his condition.

"By all odds the most famous athlete on the field, Owens will also be the least fortunate," the article said. "He attained a degree of proficiency in his sport far above the reach of any Dodger or Red in baseball when he won four gold medals at the Olympic Games." The newspaper added: "Tonight Owens will be on display for half an hour. He will give handicaps to ball players in the 100-yard dash. He will skip over a flight of low hurdles and try to beat ball players who are running 120 yards on the flat. He will give an exhibition of broad jumping. The holder of six world records will be one of the trained seals rounding out the show. It's a terrific comedown, but it's a living."

The Hypocrisy of Heroism

There is the hypocrisy of heroism.

Last week [October 17, 2012] Nike announced that it was jumping off the Lance Armstrong bandwagon.

Why did Nike abandon Armstrong and not Tiger Woods or [basketball player] Kobe Bryant?

Nike said it was betrayed and misled, though certainly no more than the world was deceived by Woods, who implied—or allowed marketers to infer—that his great character was at the root of his athletic success. Armstrong was simply an illusionist: he told us he was riding up the sides of mountains without chemical help.

The reasons Nike stuck with Woods and abandoned Armstrong have more to do with money. Woods and Bryant are still making loads of it for the corporation. Woods remains golf's greatest attraction; Bryant has won N.B.A. championships and, according to Forbes, is the second most highly compensated athlete behind Woods.

But Armstrong has no more mountains to climb, no more Tour de Frances to win. Publicly humiliated, his reputation shattered, Armstrong has no value to any of the companies who backed him, including his own, apparently. Last week, [October 17, 2012] Armstrong announced he was stepping down as the chairman of Livestrong, his cancer foundation. At least Armstrong is alive to defend what is left of his reputation.

The Tragedy of Heroism

Finally, there is the tragedy of heroism.

[Former college football coach] Joe Paterno was revered at Penn State. He was admired and celebrated by journalists as the coach who did it the right way, who graduated his athletes and stressed character. But Paterno was fired for his role in the [assistant coach] Jerry Sandusky child sexual-abuse scandal. The university's board of trustees determined that Paterno should have and could have done more to protect the children whom Sandusky abused. Will all the good that Paterno accomplished be buried with him, overshadowed by the scandal?

Sport has no enduring worth unless attached to a set of higher values.

At the funeral of Julius Caesar in Shakespeare's play, Mark Antony says, "The evil that men do lives after them; the good is oft interred with their bones."

But must this be?

Armstrong did overcome cancer and has, in fact, raised millions of dollars for cancer research. Paterno did in fact graduate players. Consider the public citizen who runs into a burning building and saves a family. Later we discover that the same citizen has been cited for domestic abuse. Should personal scandals negate the good deed? The lives are still saved.

Sport has no enduring worth unless attached to a set of higher values.

A few years after Barkley made his comments about role models, Bill Bradley, the former senator and Knicks star, wrote a wonderful book, *Values of the Game*. It focused on basketball, but the values Bradley outlined form the foundation of all sports: passion, discipline, selflessness, respect, courage, leadership, responsibility, resilience.

Given the realities of social media, forgiveness and resilience are far more valuable than heroism.

There is nothing heroic about the athlete who plays hurt and performs brilliantly, the hitter who smacks the game-winning home run or the kicker who makes the winning field goal on the last play of the game.

Perhaps we can agree, moving forward, that our sports heroes do good things but do not have to be good people.

In her book on heroism, *Heroes, Saviors, Traitors, and Supermen: A History of Hero Worship*, Lucy Hughes-Hallett argues: "Virtue is not a necessary qualification for hero status; a hero is not a role model. On the contrary, it is of the essence of a hero to be unique and therefore inimitable."

The American hero is part of our mythology, a relic of days gone by. Dead and unnecessary.

Charles Barkley may have had it right, after all.

4

African American Athletes Have a Right and a Duty to Be Role Models

Mike Tillery

Mike Tillery is the founder and former editor-in-chief of the sports blog The Starting Five. *He is a contributing writer for* The Nation, SLAM *magazine,* The New York Times, *and Sacramento* magazine.

Although society has come a long way since the turbulent 1960s, when African American athletes such as Jim Brown, Muhammad Ali, Bill Russell, and Kareem Abdul-Jabbar were outspoken advocates for racial equality, today's black athletes still face racism from franchise owners and management, fans, and the media, who often depict them as greedy, undisciplined, and immoral. However, athletes today have more of an opportunity than their forebears did to combat these perceptions using social media and the numerous twenty-four-hour sports news networks, and thus must take it upon themselves to do so.

In 1968, amid the fires of the Black Freedom Struggle, *Sports Illustrated's* Jack Olsen wrote the groundbreaking and controversial piece "The Black Athlete—A Shameful Story." It was an overview of black athletes in revolt. At the time, the best athletes in the country—Jim Brown [football player], Bill Russell [basketball player], Lew Alcindor (soon-to-be Kareem

Mike Tillery, "The Black Athlete Today," *The Nation*, vol. 293, no. 7/8, August 15–22, 2011, p. 34. Copyright © 2011 by The Nation. Reprinted with permission from the August 15, 2011 issue of The Nation. For subscription information, call 1-800-333-8536. Portions of each week's Nation magazine can be accessed at http://www.thenation.com.

Abdul-Jabbar) [basketball player] and Muhammad Ali [boxer]—were a part of this revolt. (There were African-American women athletes who would have been a part of this movement, but they found themselves shut out.) In addition, a group of African-American athletes, led by Tommie Smith [football player and track and field athlete], Lee Evans [track and field athlete], and John Carlos [track and field athlete], were threatening to boycott that year's Olympic Games in Mexico City. Olsen—for better or worse—focused on the shock felt by mainstream white sports fans that such a revolt would even be necessary.

As Olsen wrote, "What is happening today amounts to a revolt by the black athlete against the framework and attitudes of American sport, and that such a thing could occur in his own pet province has astonished the white sports follower. The reason for the astonishment is that the man in the grandstand knows nothing about the Negro athlete whom he professes to understand, appreciate and ennoble as a symbol of the enlightened attitude of the world of sport toward segregation and intolerance. A wall of ignorance and unfounded suppositions is shielding the fan from the realities of the black athlete's background and his hopes."

Fast-forward to 2011: in an era of twenty-four-hour sports media, the dynamics described by Olsen are profoundly different but also disturbingly similar. Cable networks and fans lining up for luxury boxes are more distanced than ever from the reality that black athletes travel through to make it to the big leagues. In an era of fantasy sports, fans dream of controlling players instead of becoming them. The players also tend to come from impoverished backgrounds, as they did forty years ago, while becoming much wealthier than their forebears. That has created a canyon between the black player and the white fan and overwhelmingly white press corps. And the latitude of that press corps to be brazenly racist is often jaw-dropping. Witness prominent ESPN national radio host Colin

Cowherd's recent assertion that (white) NFL commissioner Roger Goodell is a "father figure" to African-American football players who never had the paternal structure and discipline that Goodell provides. Somehow he still has a job. This kind of easy ignorance about and antipathy toward African-American athletes has created a new phenomenon: the black athletic boogeyman.

The Black Athletic Boogeyman

Websites now compete for attention by parading the latest boogeyman—whether it's [baseball player] Barry Bonds, [football player] Rashard Mendenhall or [football player] James Harrison—before a largely white fan base. All three of these athletes found controversy, but for profoundly different reasons. Bonds has long been suspected of being a steroid user. Mendenhall argued on Twitter that rejoicing over [terrorist leader] Osama bin Laden's death was barbaric. Harrison posed for a magazine with two of his guns and unleashed a stream of invective at Goodell (calling him a "faggot"). Yet despite the vast differences in the legality and morality of these acts, each athlete was pilloried in the press in a similar way: as a symbol of the moral degeneracy of black athletes. It's twenty-first-century racism, and sports celebrity is used to make it palatable. After all, they're rich, right?

Today there is no black freedom struggle—no movement—to challenge this state of affairs. That makes athletes hesitant to speak out. But unlike in 1968, when publications like *Sports Illustrated* dominated public opinion, athletes today have the financial and media power to challenge the way they're depicted in the press. Social media have also had an empowering effect. Athletes can speak out more easily and thus play a role in how "the black athlete" is perceived. In the words of NBA [National Basketball Association] player Etan Thomas, this "can be seen as a burden or blessing."

"Athletes have a big responsibility," NBA guard Deron Williams said to me. "They have a big audience. If they have an opinion and want it heard, there's no better way to do it. We have the media outlets available to get your voice heard, so you go ahead and speak on it."

Athletes need to realize that they can shape their own image much more successfully than athletes of previous generations could.

Athletes Must Speak Out

The question is how to use this platform to make change and not just become the whipping boy of the moment. NBA all-star Grant Hill, now pushing 40, told me the following: "I think from where we are now to when my dad first entered the whole realm of professional sports, obviously we were better suited. We have more control of our careers. We have more of a voice. Whether it's in social media or what have you, the African-American athlete has more wealth and more power. In terms of social consciousness, times are a little different than what Jim Brown, Kareem Abdul-Jabbar and Muhammad Ali had to go through. Because of those athletes, things are a little different. The main difference is power—the ability to move from team to team and also speak your mind."

The question is, How can more athletes be encouraged to speak their mind? One who preferred to remain anonymous said to me, "I don't speak out because all I'll be doing is giving material to the local sports-radio assholes. Why would I want to make their lives easier?"

We need a movement to defend African-American athletes and their right to speak out, so they will feel they have a base of support. But even more critically, athletes need to realize that they can shape their own image much more successfully than athletes of previous generations could. The perpetual news cycle needs material. We can feed the beast, or the beast will feed on us, and if it does, we'll be stuck in a cycle where athletic success fuels rather than challenges racism in America. Too many athletes do too much good to have it swallowed up, unreported and forgotten.

5

Female Athletes Empower Young Women Despite Objectification

Joe Posnanski

Joe Posnanski is an award-winning columnist for NBC Sports and former senior columnist for Sports Illustrated. *He was twice named the best sports columnist in America by the Associated Press Sports Editors (APSE) in 2002 and 2005, and in 2012 he was named National Sportswriter of the Year by the National Sportscasters and Sportswriters Association. His books* The Machine: A Hot Team, a Legendary Season, and a Heart-Stopping World Series—The Story of the 1975 Cincinnati Reds *(2009) and* Paterno *(2012) were both* New York Times *best sellers.*

Female auto racing driver Danica Patrick is simultaneously celebrated and criticized for embracing her status as a sex symbol while breaking gender barriers in the male-dominated sport of auto racing. But for young female sports fans, such controversies are inconsequential. Patrick is a role model simply because she has broadened the realm of possibilities for female participation in professional sports.

Every so often—maybe once or twice a week—Katie, the eight-year-old, will mention that Danica Patrick once won a race in Japan. Katie does not need an excuse to unload this little fact on us. We could be talking about her school spelling words, how she can't find her shoes, a surprising turn of events on the cooking show "Sweet Genius" or tentative plans for her next birthday party.*

Katie is ALWAYS planning her next birthday party. The minute this year's party ends, she begins working on next year's birthday party.

It really doesn't matter at all what we were talking about.

"You know, Danica Patrick won a race in Japan," she will say.

"Is that right?" I will ask for the 438th time.

"Yes," Katie will say. "You didn't know that? You're a sportswriter. You should know that. I read it in my book."

Ah, yes, the book, "Danica Patrick (Amazing Athlete)" is a staple of Katie's library—along with all the Weird School books with names like "Miss Daisy Is Crazy" and "Miss Cooney Is Looney" and "Mr. Klutz Is Nuts." Katie will pick up "Danica Patrick (Amazing Athlete)" whenever she is looking for a little inspiration or just when she remembers that she has not read it in a little while. See, Danica Patrick is one of Katie's big role models. Anyway, that's what Katie tells me.

It's easy to forget, though, what those words—role model—mean to an eight-year-old girl . . . or at least what they mean to MY eight-year-old girl. Obviously, Patrick has been very much in the news. She won the pole for this weekend's [February 2013] Daytona 500, [National Association for Stock Car Auto Racing] NASCAR's marquee race, and everyone knows that she was the first woman to do that, the first woman to come close to doing that. It is a remarkable achievement for any young driver, man or woman, to win the Daytona pole. Sunday, at the Daytona 500 race itself, she could make all kinds of history—if she were to beat the 42 men in the biggest race, well, the mind boggles at how big a sports story it would become.

Of course, with Patrick there's always more going on than just sports. She is finishing a divorce, and she has started dating NASCAR driver Ricky Stenhouse Jr. ("I feel like I'm on the bachelorette," she tells reporters). She is very pretty, and knows it, and does suggestive commercials for Go Daddy as well as less evocative ones for various other companies. She is a blend of wildly contrasting fates. She is a talented driver who expects to be taken seriously—a challenge for any woman who competes against men. She is a nationally famous super-star who has not yet won a major race in America. She is also a sex symbol who protests being a sex symbol while embracing being a sex symbol—she walks that tightrope with confidence.

Broader Horizons

None of these things matter whatsoever to my daughter Katie . . . not even her winning the pole at Daytona. Her infatuation with Danica Patrick is about something much simpler and plainer.

"Do only men play football?" Katie asked me one Sunday when I was watching NFL [National Football League] games on television.

So much of childhood is about crossing out what's unrealistic.

"Do only men play baseball?" she asked one afternoon when I was watching the Kansas City Royals playing.

"Do girls play golf too?" she asked when I was watching some [Professional Golfers' Association] PGA Tournament go-ing on somewhere in America.

These questions were not pleas from a little girl who wanted to make a point or make a stand. They were questions about possibilities. [Comedian] Jerry Seinfeld tells this great joke: "When men are growing up and reading about Batman, Superman and Spiderman, these are not fantasies. These are options." As a little kid, I think, every door is wide open, every dream a chance, every fantasy a reality, and you only slowly come to understand that maybe you won't learn to fly, maybe you aren't a music prodigy who can play a song after hearing it once, maybe the Major Leagues is not realistic because you can't even hit the fastball of the kid who lives two houses down.

So much of childhood is about crossing out what's unrealistic. It doesn't come in a single bolt, but slowly, very, slowly, day by day by day, the future comes into sharper focus and the fuzzy world where anything's possible loses just a little bit of its wonder.

For my daughters, particularly Katie, I have found, this is even more true. Seinfeld's superheroes, the most famous superheroes, are all men*. Of course, there has never been a woman president. There has never been a woman in the Major Leagues. There has never been a woman quarterback in the NFL or a woman coach of a major men's team or, well, you can go on and on and on.

*Yes, of course I know, there are lots of superheroines like Wonder Woman with her invisible plane and Catwoman with her baffling and conflicted loyalties and various other lesser superhero lights.

These too-obvious facts are not too obvious to an 8-year-old girl. She learns them slowly, reluctantly. She reaches for something. When Katie watched the U.S. women's 4x100 relay team break the world record, she was utterly enthralled. It has been months, but even now if you ask Katie what she wants to be when she grows up she will talk about being a teacher or a singer or a writer or something like that, it changes all the time, but she always plans to run the anchor leg of the Olympic relay.

In the end, that is why Danica Patrick matters to Katie. It isn't that Katie wants to be a race car driver. She doesn't even ride her bicycle much. But . . . it's possible. Two beautiful words. It's. Possible.

It's possible because Danica Patrick is a race car driver. It's possible because she races with the best. That's what matters to Katie. She doesn't get the GoDaddy commercials, and she doesn't know anything about Danica Patrick's personal life. She doesn't understand the nuances of NASCAR or even what a pole position means. She doesn't have too many of Patrick's accomplishments memorized; she only knows that Patrick liked racing little cars when she was small and was raised to believe she could beat anybody and, yes, she won that race in Japan.*

*The Indy Japan 300.

People talk often about role models letting us down . . . there has been plenty of that the last few months. But it depends on what you want from those role models.

And here's a beautiful thing: Patrick innately understands all this. No, she doesn't talk much about it, and she doesn't spend a lot of time talking about women's rights or girl power. But it's always there, it's a part of her, underneath the hype and endorsements and competitive hunger. And every now and again it will come out like it did this week when she said: "(Parents) can have that conversation with their kid about you can do anything you want and being different doesn't, by any means, not allow you to follow your dreams. I love to think that conversation happens in households because of something I do."

People talk often about role models letting us down . . . there has been plenty of that the last few months. But it depends on what you want from those role models. Danica Patrick cannot let down Katie because Katie doesn't care about her personal life or her various choices. "Why do you like Danica Patrick so much?" I ask Katie.

"Because she's pretty and she races cars," Katie says.

Obviously, adults expect so much more from Danica Patrick. Obviously, Patrick expects so much more from herself. She has a chance this weekend—and next weekend and the weekend after that—to break ground and take checkered flags and sell web hosting by flaunting her attractiveness. But, through the eyes of an 8-year-old girl, she has already done enough to be a role model. She has made Katie's sky just a little bit wider with just a few more stars.

6

Athletes Can Be Leaders in Ending Homophobia

Brendon Ayanbadejo

Brendon Ayanbadejo is a linebacker for the Super Bowl champion Baltimore Ravens and an ambassador for Athlete Ally, a nonprofit organization committed to ending homophobia in sports.

Professional athletes are in a unique position to foster a culture of inclusiveness both within sports and in society in general. Athletes must take a stand against homophobia and voice their support for playing alongside openly gay athletes so that the sports world will no longer be "the last closet in America." The principles of sportsmanship and teamwork should be extended to all athletes, regardless of their sexual orientation.

The trailer for the upcoming film "42" [released April 12, 2013] begins with a silhouetted baseball player walking down the tunnel toward the dugout. A voice says: "I don't know who he is, or where he is, but he's coming." The scene captures the anticipation of Jackie Robinson crossing the Major League Baseball color barrier. That moment just before history is made is a moment that sure feels a lot like now, as we wait for the arrival of the first openly gay man in U.S. major professional team sports. [National Basketball Association (NBA) basketball player Jason Collins made his homosexuality public on April 29, 2013.]

Just like Jackie, the breakthrough gay athlete will be a courageous individual going it alone in uncharted territory. But, also like Jackie, he will have backup—and hopefully more of it.

One of the seminal moments of Jackie Robinson's first season with the Brooklyn Dodgers was when teammate Pee Wee Reese put his arm around Jackie during a game and then faced the crowd. The message was clear: teammates are teammates. Brothers. Reese wasn't a civil rights advocate. But he wasn't merely a good guy either. Reese was exactly what the codes of sportsmanship expected him to be, someone who knew what was right and did it despite the risks. Simply put, he was an ally.

I know that there are plenty of good men in the NFL [National Football League]. I am fortunate to play alongside them as a member of the Super Bowl XLVII champion Baltimore Ravens. Together the Ravens became world champions. Together we can be more than Super Bowl winners. Together athletes in all four of our country's major sports leagues—the NFL, MLB [Major League Baseball], NHL [National Hockey League] and NBA—can be more than good men. Since human rights are far more important than sports, we need to be Athlete Allies . . . who are willing to leverage our social capital and all that goes with it—like fans, endorsement deals and more—to stand up for a larger purpose.

As leaders and even role models for millions of young people across the globe, professional athletes have the ability to fundamentally eliminate prejudice from our sport and live up to the incredible privilege we enjoy.

That's why I began advocating for marriage equality four years ago. As the child of a Nigerian dad and Irish-American mom, I was raised to believe that, in America, our differences don't matter and discrimination is wrong. During my career in the NFL, I've watched LGBT [lesbian, gay, bisexual, and transgender] Americans struggle to make gains in legislatures, schools and boardrooms around the country. Since I first signed with the [Atlanta] Falcons in 1999, Wall Street and corporate America have worked to create internal departments and networks focused on LGBT diversity and inclusion. The largest companies in the world have signed on to legal briefs in support of marriage rights for same-sex couples and CEOs [chief executive officers] have publicly spoken out for LGBT rights. What's even more inspiring is that, after decades of discrimination against gay and lesbian members of the United States military, President [Barack] Obama ended "don't ask, don't tell." The president made history again in his inaugural address, when he called for equal rights for gay and lesbian Americans—including the right to marry whomever they love.

The Last Closet in America

With these successes piling up and progress on the rise, an issue closer to home comes more sharply in focus: the sports world—my world—is the last closet in America.

There are many reasons why no gay athlete has come out in the NFL, NBA, NHL or MLB, most of which are likely to go away with support and acceptance from the straight community. As leaders and even role models for millions of young people across the globe, professional athletes have the ability to fundamentally eliminate prejudice from our sport and live up to the incredible privilege we enjoy.

At its best, sports do not discriminate. If you are young or old, tall or short, male or female, gay or straight, all that really matters is how well you play and contribute to your team.

The NFL, MLB, NHL and NBA should and can be leaders against discrimination. Whether you're a commissioner, an athlete, a coach or a fan, your voice will let every kid out there know that there is a place for him or her in sports. We all can be ourselves and still compete with dignity and at the highest level.

This is our time and our cause. Everything we know as athletes, teammates, spokesmen and vehicles of American pastimes compels us toward the kind of action and camaraderie we saw from Pee Wee Reese nearly 66 years ago. It's as simple as putting our arm around the shoulder of another athlete. It's a gesture; it's a pledge; it's solidarity at its most basic. Our Jackie is coming. We need to pave the way.

7

Christian Athletes Set an Example of Humility

Bryan Cribb

Bryan Cribb is an assistant professor of Christian studies at Anderson University in Anderson, South Carolina.

Prominent Christian athletes, including football player Tim Tebow and basketball player Jeremy Lin, are notable not just for their athletic accomplishments but for their humility in the face of adulation. Such humility, grounded in their Christian faith, makes them and other Christian athletes powerful role models and valuable ambassadors for Christianity around the world.

Have you caught Linsanity yet? Unless you live life with sports blinders, you probably have at least noticed the meteoric rise of Jeremy Lin, starting point guard of the New York Knicks as of only a week or so ago [February 4, 2012. Lin has since been traded to the Houston Rockets.]

On Valentine's evening, this improbable hero again amazed the watching world. Lin drained a last-second 3-pointer to win the sixth-straight game for the Knicks since Lin—a perpetual benchwarmer for his brief NBA [National Basketball Association] career and only the fourth NBA player ever from Harvard—took over as team leader. Thrust into the starting lineup due to injuries to more high-profile and highly paid players, Lin has set the ever-combustible media market in the Big Apple ablaze. The Asian American, who until recently went unrecognized even by Knicks security guards, now has spawned the highest TV ratings in recent memory for the team and galvanized the city.

What makes Lin even more intriguing, however, is his forthright Christian faith.

Labeled the "Taiwanese Tebow" by sports journalists, Lin has not shied from expressing his faith on the court, through the Internet, and in other forums. And he seems genuinely grounded in the faith. A recent Religion News Service article quoted him saying in a recent post-game interview, "I'm just thankful to God for everything. Like the Bible says, 'God works in all things for the good of those who love Him.'"

The article describes Lin's desire to play "godly basketball." As his longtime pastor asserts about him, "Very early in his life he decided to pay heed to the call of Christ to take up the cross daily and follow after him."

In an online testimony recently, Lin quotes well-known pastor/author John Piper regarding the supremacy of Christ over sports and success. Lin then states, "When Paul wrote in Philippians to press on for an upward prize, he was living for that, and it made his life meaningful (Philippians 3:15). And I realized I had to learn to do the same. I had to learn to stop chasing the perishable prizes of this earth, I had to stop chasing personal glory, I had to learn how to give my best effort to God and trust him with the results. I have to learn to have enough faith to trust in His grace and to trust in His sovereign and perfect plan. I had to submit my will, my desires, my dreams—give it all up to God and say, 'Look, I am going to give my best effort, go on the court and play every day for you, and I'm going to let you take care of the rest.' This is something I struggle with every day. . . . Playing for great stats is nice, but that satisfaction—that happiness—is only from game to game. It's temporary."

Wow!

Of course, all of these characteristics remind us of Tim Tebow, the Denver Broncos quarterback [Tebow was subsequently traded to the New York Jets and released after the 2012–2013 season], former Heisman [Trophy] winner, and outspoken Christian, who led his team on an improbable run to the NFL [National Football League] playoffs, even as naysayers decried his passing ability and doubted his capability to quarterback his team.

In the face of such scorn, Tebow consistently exhibited Christlike humility, grace and determined leadership. And the world took note.

With Lin and Tebow, we seem to have a new breed of Christian athlete—orthodox and exemplary, in addition to being outspoken and excellent in their God-given roles.

Now, I come from an era when Christian sports heroes might thank God for a win or mention praying or talk about being a Christian in general terms. I would often excitedly tell friends about sports figures who avowed faith publicly. But then I would witness these same Christian stars fall in some heinous sin or, just as bad, make an appearance on Trinity Broadcasting Network with sequin donned "prosperity gospel" hawkers, talking about God's "blessing" on their careers.

But with Lin and Tebow, we seem to have a new breed of Christian athlete—orthodox and exemplary, in addition to being outspoken and excellent in their God-given roles.

I mean, how refreshing was it to see Tebow recently turn down an opportunity to speak at a conference/rally that was to be hosted by the well-known prosperity proponents Rod Parsley and Kenneth Copeland! Tebow rightly recognized what is the true Gospel and what is, as Paul states, a patently false "contrary to the one we preached to you" (Galatians 1:8).

A New Era of Christian Athletes

Yes, I believe Tebow and Lin represent excellent examples of a new era of Christian athletes who are unashamed, as well as grounded in the historic faith once for all delivered to the saints.

What makes these two athletes such powerful witnesses is not just their fame and not just their "on their frontlets" faith. It is their character and leadership and excellence in what they do for a living.

And they are having an impact on secular culture—if anything by bringing Christianity out of the realm of private expression and into the realm of public discourse.

I almost wrecked my car a few weeks ago after hearing two very secular hosts of a Fox sports radio program argue over a correct Scripture reference. One of the hosts apparently looked it up on the spot and found the quotation. The source of this odd discussion? Tebow, of course.

What makes these two athletes such powerful witnesses is not just their fame and not just their "on their frontlets" faith. It is their character and leadership and excellence in what they do for a living. Seeing Lin selflessly delivering key passes, diving for every loose ball, chest bumping his teammates. . . . Seeing Tebow inspiring a rather uninspiring Denver Broncos supporting cast to play beyond their ability. . . . To use a hip term, these actions "represent." Specifically, they model Christ to the watching world.

Of course, it doesn't hurt that these two seem to represent with a well-grounded faith, as well. But it does show all Christians an example of how a Christian may impact his or her respective circle of influence with positive outlooks, energetic leadership, selfless service, humility in the wake of accomplishment, and unashamed witness whenever the opportunity presents.

This doesn't mean that you need to "Tebow" the next time you get a raise. But I do believe that open witness backed by impeccable character and orthodox theology is a powerful evangelistic tool in any setting—whether on the football field or the basketball court, or just in your cubicle or by the copy machine.

Christian "Linsanity" can happen anywhere. And we need more unsung, everyday Tebows and Lins for the cause of Christ.

8

Christian Athletes Are Not Role Models

Mark Galli

Mark Galli is senior managing editor of Christianity Today *and the author of a number of books on Christian theology. He writes a regular column for* Christianity Today, *"Soul Work," in which he applies Christian ideas to recent news stories.*

Two of the star players in the 2012 Super Bowl, Baltimore Ravens linebacker Ray Lewis and San Francisco 49ers quarterback Colin Kaepernick, are very public with their Christian beliefs, leading many in the religious community to hold them up as role models. A closer look at these athletes' pasts and motives reveals that they are imperfect and in no way fit to serve as moral leaders. Christian athletes should instead present themselves as sinners in search of redemption.

John Kruk never looked like much of an athlete. He was a first baseman for the Philadelphia Phillies in the late 1980s and early 1990s, but as a teammate put it, he looked like a guy who drove a beer truck. His many diets were never able to trim his belly—"Don't worry," he once said. "I can always put the weight back on. Quickly." Despite his poor physique and bad habits he was a consistently good hitter, and ended his career with a lifetime .300 batting average.

One time he was sitting in a restaurant, eating a big meal while downing a couple of beers and smoking a cigarette, when a woman approached his table. She recognized him but said she was shocked, because she thought that he should be in training and that a professional athlete should take better care of himself.

Kruk leaned back and said, "I ain't an athlete, lady, I'm a baseball player."

The story reminds me of another quote, this one from basketball hall of famer Charles Barkley. He was one of the most dominating power forwards of his day (1990s), who used his strength and aggressiveness to intimidate opponents. He had no patience for those who believed athletes should be role models for kids. "A million guys can dunk a basketball in jail," he once said. "Should they be role models?"

As we come to another Super Bowl [Super Bowl XLVII], we Christians note that the leaders of each team are devout believers—Colin Kaepernick on the [San Francisco] 49ers and Ray Lewis on the [Baltimore] Ravens. Like any group with a strong self-identity, we Christians are proud that members of our tribe are star players in this national extravaganza. Not unexpectedly, when Christians become prominent in athletics, we are tempted to turn them into role models. We want them, like the lady wanted of John Kruk, to be models of athleticism, and like Charles Barkley comments, to be models of morality, as well.

But I suspect Charles Barkley had it right. Even Christian athletes, in the end, make for poor moral role models.

Glorious Athletes in Action

Our desire to lift them up as models of athleticism, morality—and religion—goes way back. The ancient Olympics were not merely athletic events but also religious festivals. The games were dedicated to the Greek god Zeus, and over time, the site of the games, Olympia, became worship central for the god of thunder. It included one of the largest Doric temples in Greece, and a 42-foot statue, made of gold and ivory, which sat on the throne of the temple. It was one of the seven wonders of the ancient world.

When we see a Christian winner on the field, we hope against hope that he is a moral winner in his life—a role model for our children, and maybe even for us.

As the ancient historian Strabo put it, the Olympian games were considered "the greatest games in the world." Indeed, they were the Super Bowls of the ancient world. While there were no commercials specially created for the event, artists would cast wondrous works of art to celebrate the games and the athleticism displayed there. The most well-known perhaps is Myron's *Diskobolos, or Discus Thrower*—a thrower frozen just before he unwinds and hurls the discus. His physique is a picture of athletic beauty, a combination of power and grace that every athlete (if not John Kruk!) strives for.

When we see that power and grace in the field of play—well, it is a thing of wonder. We're witnessing human glory (that glory that is just a little less than the angels—Psalm 8). When we witness such a sight, it's almost impossible not to hope that this same human being might be a specimen of excellence in other arenas. Thus is born in us the desire for the athlete to be a moral role model.

As a society, we know better. There may have been a time when the immoral escapades of athletes were discretely ignored by journalists, but that time is no more. What amazes us today is not to discover that an athlete is narcissistic, greedy, and selfish; a philanderer, a drug addict, or even a murderer. It's when we find one who appears humble and morally upright. Thus our culture's fascination with [football player] Tim Tebow—an "oddball" in today's athletic culture.

For Christians, such moments feel like vindication: See, Christianity does make a difference! And when we see a Christian winner on the field, we hope against hope that he is a moral winner in his life—a role model for our children, and maybe even for us.

If you're like me, you want to feel that way about the two devout Christian stars who will take the field this Sunday. But that's a stretch.

Take Ray Lewis, whom sports writer Frank Deford described like this,

> He is not, shall we say, quite the exemplary family man, having sired six children with a variety of women. He was indicted for murder in the year 2000, turned state's evidence and pled guilty to obstruction of justice. And, of course, he can be a brutal player—witness the monstrous illegal monstrous hit he pummeled the [New England] Patriots' Aaron Hernandez with in the AFC [American Football Conference] championship.

Add to that the strong evidence, as reported in this week's *Sports Illustrated*, that he took a banned substance earlier this season, and you get the picture. Or I should say the lack of a picture of moral rectitude.

At first glance, Colin Kaepernick seems like a better candidate for a role model. He was raised in a Christian home, and has Scripture verses tattooed over his body. As he told former NFL [National Football League] star quarterback Kurt Warner, "My first tattoo was a scroll on my right arm, Psalm 18:39. . . . It's just my way of showing everybody that this is what I believe in."

Well, except that the verses on his body are not exactly testimonies to humility or the grace of Christ, but seem designed to inspire aggressive play. Psalm 18:39 reads, "You armed me with strength for battle; you humbled my adversaries before me." Another tattoo, from Psalm 27:3, reads "Though an army besiege me, my heart will not fear; though war break out against me, even then I will be confident."

These verses are, in fact, apt descriptions of how this guy plays: he's fearless, determined, bellicose (prone to sling out four-letter words at his opponents), and extremely competitive. Not that there's a problem with being competitive—well, except when it is driven by pride. And Kaepernick's case it is. As a recent cover story in *Sports Illustrated* put it,

> The truth is, beneath the serene, smiling exterior, Kap is still upset. He's angry at the college coaches who didn't find him worthy of a scholarship; at the NFL teams that needed a quarterback and didn't draft him; at the San Francisco fans who preferred [former starter Alex] Smith.

Kaepernick says, "I had a lot to prove," explaining, "A lot of people doubted me and my ability to lead this time."

The most wondrous things we're seeing on the field are not glorious athletes but graced sinners.

Well, that's understandable, but let's face it: it's a desire driven by the need to justify oneself before others. It's called pride, and it's one of the seven deadly sins—a sin that every one of us is very familiar with, no?

Signs of Grace

This gives us a clue about what we should be looking for in our Christian athletes—nothing more, nor less, than we look for in ourselves: signs of God's grace.

The Christian athlete, like any athlete in top condition and training, is a picture of athletic grace, to be sure. We can glorify our Creator for giving some men and women such extraordinary abilities for us to behold. But beyond that, we're looking at typically weak, selfish, prideful people, subject to the same temptations that we succumb to. They carry about with them a body, however glorious for the moment, that is subject to decay, with a heart desperately wicked (Jer. 17:9). *Scoundrels* is another word to describe us. *Sinners* is the biblical word.

And yet. These scoundrels—like us—are the very objects of God's mercy. It is for such that Christ died. As he put it, he didn't come for the role models, but for those who have failed to be role models (Luke 5:32). The most wondrous things we're seeing on the field are not glorious athletes but graced sinners.

Any athlete who begins to imagine that he is, in fact, a role model, would be wise to remember Jesus' parable of the Role Model and the Scoundrel in Luke 18:

> Two men went up into the megachurch to pray, one a Role Model, and the other a Scoundrel. The Role Model, standing by himself and yet in clear view of the ESPN cameras, prayed thus: "God, I thank you that I am not like other athletes—self-centered, adulterers, and drug addicts, or even like that Scoundrel. I work out twice a day, I give my all, on and off the field, to be an example to others." But the Scoundrel, standing far off away from the microphones, would not even lift up his eyes, but wept, saying, "God, be merciful to me, a scoundrel!"

Jesus seemed to think the latter was the real role model.

Might I suggest a line for our favorite Christian athletes to use when people want to make them into something they are not?

"Hey, I ain't no role model; I'm just a scoundrel. . . ."

9

Paralympians Are Inspirations for All

James Mastro, Christopher Ahrens, and Nathan Statton.

James Mastro is a seven-time paralympian who has earned ten medals in four different sports and is a professor in the department of professional and physical education at Bemidji State University in Bemidji, Minnesota. Christopher Ahrens is a member of the US Paralympics soccer team and is an adapted physical education teacher in the San Diego Unified School District. Nathan Statton is a graduate assistant at Bemidji State University.

Paralympians and athletes with disabilities are true role models, not only for the disabled, but for all. Students in particular can benefit from learning about Paralympians and their ability to persevere in the face of obstacles.

For the purpose of this article, a role model is a person or challenge that inspires an individual to go beyond what is expected of him or her and to reach a specific goal. Role models can exemplify motivation, passion, and a genuine love of their life's work. All students need role models, and Paralympic sport athletes can be just that, especially for students with disabilities.

Pioneers in disability sport did not always have role models to look up to or emulate. It was not until the establish-

James Mastro, Christopher Ahrens, and Nathan Statton. "Using Role Models to Help Celebrate Paralympic Sport," *JOPERD—The Journal of Physical Education, Recreation & Dance*, vol. 83, no. 4 (April 2012), pp. 28–31, Taylor & Francis. Reprinted by permission of the publisher (Taylor & Francis, Ltd, http://www.tandf.co.uk/journals).

ment of organizations such as the United States Association of Blind Athletes (USABA) or the National Wheelchair Athletic Association that role models and mentors became accessible to future generations. Role models, people who are inspirational, heroes, and mentors are now abundant throughout disability sport.

One of the authors has defined a role model as

> a person that people can look up to and respect. This isn't limited to just professional or athletic achievement but how they live their lives. I feel as though Paralympic athletes can serve as role models for students both with and without disabilities. Generally, Paralympic athletes are not money-driven individuals, but truly participate for love of the sport.

This article describes how disability sport role models can be used in a physical education Paralympic unit.

Using Role Models in Physical Education

There are a variety of ways of using role models to educate and inspire students about disability sport in the physical education curriculum.

Teaching students a disability sport that they can excel in is probably the best way of incorporating the Paralympics in general physical education classes.

Speakers. Some athletes with disabilities are available to make presentations or speeches. They can be contacted through their disability sport group or through the individual athlete's web page. Topics could include empowerment, diversity, acceptance, stigma, handicapism, and stereotypes.

Demonstration Events. On a Paralympic sport day at school, it would be exciting for professional athletes or even a team (i.e., wheelchair basketball, Paralympic soccer, goalball) to come and participate in the program. Local teams that compete in a Paralympic sport are often willing to provide a demonstration of their skills and talents.

Helping to Teach the Sport. Teaching students a disability sport that they can excel in is probably the best way of incorporating the Paralympics in general physical education classes. Professional athletes with disabilities could come to school and help teach sports like goalball, wheelchair basketball, wheelchair soccer, quad rugby, beep baseball, bocce, track and field, and others.

Field Trips. It might be possible to take the class on a field trip to a competition (e.g., a wheelchair basketball tournament) and have students interview the athletes before or after the game.

Disabled Veterans as Athletic Role Models

Marine Sergeant Carlos Leon, a young, fit soccer athlete, enlisted in 2004 right out of high school. Carlos returned home to base in Hawaii for a short rest and recovery period after his first deployment to Iraq. While there, he was injured in a fluke diving accident that fractured the C5 section of his spine. His injury left him unable to move for nine months, and he underwent major rehabilitation. His mental toughness and determination helped him through recovery, and soon he was propelling a manual wheelchair. His recreation therapist then approached him about an opportunity. Carlos had been invited to a Paralympic Military Sport Camp in San Diego, and there he found his future in competitive athletics. He met an athlete in the sport of field events (shot put, discus, etc.) who later became a mentor and coach. The staff saw great potential in Carlos and encouraged him to consider training on a full-time basis. He got his big break in 2007, when he made the national team and traveled to Rio de Janeiro for the Para-Panamerican Games. Carlos was also selected for a new program within the U.S. Olympic Committee, Paralympic Division, called the Veterans Performance Program, which later became the U.S. Paralympic Military Sports Program. He and one other veteran trained full time at Lakeshore Foundation in Birmingham, Alabama, leading up to the 2008 Paralympic Games in Beijing. All his hard work and dedication paid off when the team was announced and his name was on the list; it was official, he would be competing on the second largest sport-event stage in the world: the Paralympic Games. To date, Carlos has competed in several national and international events. He is currently training full time in Ft. Lauderdale, Florida, and although he had been primarily training for the shot put and discus events, he has found a new love in the sport of triathlon.

On Christmas Day in 2005, Army Sergeant Noah Galloway woke up in a room at Walter Reed Army Medical Center [in Washington, DC]. His parents revealed to him that he had been unconscious for several days and had made the trek from Iraq to Landsthul, Germany, and then to Walter Reed. The last thing he remembered was driving his humvee in the dead of night. He did not see the trip wire across the road, which ignited two hidden 155-mm artillery shells and threw his vehicle into a ravine. The explosion took his left arm above the elbow and his left leg above the knee, but it did not take away his drive and tenacity that helped propel him through the next months of recovery. When Noah enlisted after the [terrorist] attacks on 9/11 [2001], he thought that being a soldier was going to be his lifelong career. After being injured, he made it a personal goal to get out of the hospital as fast as possible and get back to his home state of Alabama. Back in Birmingham, he was introduced to a local organization called the Lakeshore Foundation. There he took part in the Lima Foxtrot Programs for Injured Military and was introduced to disability sport through one of their extended weekend programs. Noah now serves as a speaker on behalf of Lakeshore, is involved in extended day-cycling trips, and most recently has traveled to Indonesia to climb Carstensz, the highest peak in Oceania. Being involved in sport and recreation has given him the opportunity to travel all across the country, meet other injured service members, and get involved in a community-based sport program. Noah's fitness is most important to him, and he has fallen in love with competitions like Warrior Dash, Barbarian Challenge, and Tough Mudder. Whether it is running 12 miles through mud and obstacles, or cycling through New York with other service members, he always says that participating in sports and recreation after injury is the reason he has progressed so much.

Using athletes with disabilities as the focus of presentations in physical education classes can benefit not only potential athletes with disabilities, but all students.

On September 2, 2006, Captain Ivan Castro was injured during a mortar attack that left him blind. After months of rehabilitation he became involved in an athletic program through the USABA and U.S. Paralympics. He now works as a recruiter and mentor, projecting a positive attitude while overcoming personal challenges. Since his injury, he has finished 11 marathons and many other distance races, including some triathlons. His goals are to participate in the Iron Man Triathlon in Hawaii, cycle across the United States, and hike the Appalachian Trail.

These three service members suffered different injuries and took very different paths; one through elite-level Paralympic sport, one through a community-based organization, and the third through national competitions. The common thread is sport, and the fact that they are all pursuing a healthy, active lifestyle despite their disabilities.

Summary

A role model is a person who inspires others to go beyond what is expected of them, an individual who exemplifies motivation, passion, and love for their life's work. There are many role models in disability sport throughout the United States. Using athletes with disabilities as the focus of presentations in physical education classes can benefit not only potential athletes with disabilities, but all students.

Reference

Sherrill, C. (2004). Adapted physical activity, recreation and sport (6th ed.). Boston: McGraw-Hill.

10

Marketers Need Stricter Moral Clauses to Police Athlete Behavior

Christopher R. Chase

Christopher R. Chase is legal counsel specializing in intellectual property, advertising, and entertainment law at Frankfurt Kurnit Klein & Selz. He has counseled major sports leagues on intellectual property and branding and is a member of the Sports Lawyers Association and the National Sports Marketing Network.

Because today's twenty-four-hour media environment places athletes at greater risk of being embroiled in scandal at some point in their career, marketers should take it upon themselves to insert broad morals clauses into endorsement contracts. Beyond traditional issues such as legal convictions, morals clauses should take into account new arenas for disreputable conduct, such as social media. Although such clauses may not necessarily convince athletes to stay out of trouble, they will allow brands to legally cut ties with controversial figures without being drawn into scandal themselves.

Now, more than ever, brands need to ensure that the morals clause in their endorsement agreements has evolved to meet the risks of a changing media world.

Recent scandals involving high-profile endorsers have shined a light on the morals clause. For example, Nike, Trek,

Oakley and others dropped pro cyclist Lance Armstrong after he was stripped of his Tour de France titles and banned for life from competitive cycling due to a "massive" doping scheme, and HanesBrands terminated NFL [National Football League] runningback Rashard Mendenhall from endorsing its Champion brand following his controversial tweets about the death of [terrorist leader] Osama Bin Laden and the terrorist attacks of September 11 [2001].

Such scandals should convince brands and their agencies to push for broader "out" clauses in any endorsement agreement.

Morals clauses often give the brand the ability to suspend or terminate the agreement, or obtain a reduction in fees, in the event that the endorser commits an act that falls within the scope of such clause. But morals clauses, which are frequently found to be enforceable by the courts, are one of the most heavily negotiated and controversial provisions in endorsement agreements.

Neither the brand nor the endorser will likely argue that a conviction or an indictment—such as [football player] Michael Vick's conviction for dog-fighting activities—does not cause the endorser to be subject to public disrepute. But headline-generating activities that are less than criminal—such as [professional golfer] Tiger Woods' marital infidelities—may still cause harm to the endorser, and by association, the brand.

The key is the tension between the brand and the endorser as to the type of publicity or activity covered by the morals clause. The brand favors broad, subjective language ("if endorser becomes, in the opinion of Company, the subject of public disrepute, contempt or scandal") that will enable it to terminate or suspend an endorser. On the other hand, the endorser favors specific, objective language ("if endorser is convicted of, or pleads guilty to, a felony") because what is a disreputable, contemptable or scandalous act in one context may be quite acceptable in another. The final negotiated language will depend on the context of the endorsement given the type of brand and the type of endorser, and, of course, the bargaining positions of the parties.

Given the different types of activities that can threaten a brand's reputation, brands and their agencies are now pushing to either include broad language in a morals clause . . . or incorporate specific language for actions that the brand deems problematic.

The very public outing of Armstrong's ongoing doping scheme by the United States Anti-Doping Agency last year provided neither an arrest, an indictment, nor a conviction. But the drama certainly subjected Armstrong to public disrepute. If the morals clauses in Armstrong's various endorsement agreements incorporated only limited specific, objective language, it's possible that the endorsed brand would have to continue to pay Armstrong despite being practically unable to use him.

Similarly, Mendenhall, whose tweets prompted Hanes-Brands to terminate his endorsement agreement with the Champion brand, did not commit a crime, yet HanesBrands believed that Mendenhall was no longer an appropriate representative of the Champion brand. Mendenhall subsequently sued HanesBrands, seeking to enforce his endorsement agreement and arguing that HanesBrands improperly terminated him. Although the morals clause in Mendenhall's endorsement agreement included broad, subjective language, the federal district court hearing his case has initially sided with Mendenhall, but the case continues [Mendenhall and Hanesbrands reached a settlement on January 17, 2013].

New Kinds of Scandals

Given the different types of activities that can threaten a brand's reputation, brands and their agencies are now pushing to either include broad language in a morals clause that would cover a number of "disreputable" activities or incorporate specific language for actions that the brand deems problematic.

For example, due to the long-held view that professional cycling involved a number of doping athletes, a brand using such an endorser may want to include failed drug tests or allegations of possession, use, or sale of banned substances as triggers for termination or suspension.

Additionally, brands concerned with the social-media presence of an endorser may seek to include language concerning the social-media activities of its endorser—ranging from the good-faith determination of the brand to what a reasonable person would deem to render the endorsement of lesser value in order to give a judge a basis for permitting the brand to cease paying or perhaps recoup a pro rata portion of the fees paid.

Of course, in the world of social media the brand should be careful to not insist on something that would be viewed negatively by the brand's own fans, such as requiring an endorser to refrain from posting about politics, religion or sex during the term of the endorsement agreement.

Because of the never-ending types of hot water an endorser may find himself or herself in, the language used by brands in endorsement agreements must evolve to cover such activities.

11

Love Versus Hate: How Fans Cope with Athletes' Transgressions

Leeja Carter

Leeja Carter is a faculty member at the Adler School of Professional Psychology in the sport and health psychology department of Temple University.

Studies have shown that, when confronted by their favorite athlete's bad behavior, sports fans utilize a number of coping mechanisms to retain their admiration for the athlete. These mechanisms include ignoring or refusing to believe the news of the athlete's misconduct (denial), forgiving the behavior outright, or gradually forgetting the transgression as the athlete works to repair his or her image. This willingness to overlook inappropriate acts is implicit in the athlete-fan relationship.

What do Alex Rodriguez, Michael Vick, and Tiger Woods all have in common? Despite being elite athletes in their relative sports, they have all publicly admitted to engaging in inappropriate behaviors, either sport, criminal, or maritally related. However, although their behaviors may have been wrong, they have all retained and, in some cases gained, fans.

As sports fans, we are more easily persuaded by the positive behaviors elite athletes engage in than the negative. When our favorite athlete is seen donating to underprivileged chil-

Leeja Carter, "'How Could You?': The Fan's Response To Athletes Behaving Badly: From Denial to Forgiving and Forgetting," *Psychology Today: The Inner Athlete*, January 4, 2011. www.psychologytoday.com/blog/the-inner-athlete. Copyright © 2011 by Leeja Carter. All rights reserved. Reproduced by permission.

dren, assisting in a literacy program, or positively contributing to the team dynamic, we find ourselves nodding our heads in agreement and confirming the goodwill of the athletic elite. Moreover, when athletes' on-court performance is consistently above average or exceeds expectations, our positive beliefs regarding the athlete or team are confirmed, allowing us to feel that athletes are worthy of our (e.g., the 'fans') admiration, respect, and praise.

However, how are fans perceptions affected when the athletic elite engages in poor or inappropriate behaviors? Moreover, why can fans retain a positive outlook towards athletes after they engage in poor or inappropriate behaviors? As fans, we are driven by the positive perceptions we hold of our athletes, which leads to the question, when considering athlete transgressions, do fans forgive, forget, or deny in order to cope with the occurrence of athletes behaving badly?

According to a recent study conducted by Adam Earnheardt (2010) exploring sport television viewers' perceptions of athletes' antisocial behaviors (p. 182), when athletes transgress, sports fans accurately appraise the athlete's behaviors as "bad." Such categorization is regardless of fans' levels of "fandom" (Earnheardt, 2010). Most fans understand good and bad behavior and know that antisocial or bad behaviors are socially unacceptable and wrong. However, despite fans comprehension of 'good' and 'bad,' fans continue to support an athlete after an inappropriate act or transgression.

Unwavering Support

One explanation can be found by dissecting the athlete-fan relationship; as fans follow their favorite sports, teams, and athletes, their allegiance is created through the daily or weekly rituals engaged in that strengthen their fan relationship and positive view of the athlete. The bonds between the fan and athlete slowly become strong, cementing the fan's dependency on sport as well as perpetuating the fan's role within the

greater sport culture. Thus, when athletes engage in bad behaviors, fans are forced to 'deal' which such situations emo-
tionally as well as cognitively, due to their loyalty to the athlete or team. Moreover, the fan's response may be a coping
mechanism designed to buffer feelings of anxiety or confusion
that may arise because of the fan's conflicting thoughts sur-
rounding the positive and negative images of the athlete.

---

*Many athletes who have engaged in bad behaviors know
the importance of rebuilding their public image. Such rebuilding is dependent on the public's selective attention
and amnesia.*

According to dissonance theory, when a discrepancy exists
between two thoughts or ideas, humans are motivated to reduce the feelings of anxiety that arise through the alteration
of behaviors, attitudes, or beliefs (Gosling, Maxime, & Oberle,
2006). In addition, individuals can also engage classic Freudian defense mechanisms in order to buffer such feelings of
anxiety. The defense mechanism of denial is a Freudian defense mechanism whereby the refusal to accept the reality or
truth of a situation, person, or event can be engaged in order
to reduce negative thoughts or feelings. A fan's denial can be
characterized as the refusal to admit an athlete's wrong behavior, damage, or the necessity of punishment in order to continue to perceive their idol in a positive light. Denial would
assist fans in alleviating the negative or troubling feelings that
arise when their athlete or team engages in a behavior that is
antisocial, inappropriate, or criminal as such feelings conflict
with their (i.e., the fan's) positive feelings of admiration, respect, and idealism held towards the athlete.

In comparison, forgiveness is the belief that in order to
'heal' and learn, the public should not pacify, but relinquish
any negative emotions towards the athlete in order to move
forward. 'Forgiving' an athlete can cause an athlete to lose

fans, as some may choose to "move on" to another athlete, team, or sport as part of their 'growing process.'

Lastly, fans can forget. Many athletes who have engaged in bad behaviors know the importance of rebuilding their public image. Such rebuilding is dependent on the public's selective attention and amnesia. For example, the NFL [National Football League] suspended former Atlanta Falcons quarterback Michael Vick for two years after being convicted for dog fighting in 2007 (Branch, 2010). Upon his reinstatement into the league, he has lead the Philadelphia Eagles to their 6th NFC [National Football Conference] East division title, for which his athletic performance and avoidance of negative attention have successfully steered him clear of bad press, allowing the public to see the good and potentially forget the bad. Moreover, if you weren't a fan of Vick, he is allowing fans to walk through that door, especially in Philadelphia, Pennsylvania. In contrast, one must highlight [professional golfer] Tiger Woods' publicized infidelities, sex addiction, and divorce, and ask how many positive behaviors, wins, or endorsements must he accrue in order to regain a positive public image partially affected by mere human amnesia?

For many sports fans, their team is their team; their player(s) is/are their player(s). When athletes engage in bad or inappropriate acts, the fan is confronted with conflicting views of the athlete. This cognitive conflict, whether conscious or unconscious, may be addressed through various methods of coping. Moreover, understanding that fans are conflicted with dual images of the athlete (after the athlete has transgressed), due to polarized images of "good" and "bad" which contend the fan's feelings of idealism, are what stimulate their need to cope.

References

1. Branch, J. (2010, November 10). As Vick soars, stigma of conviction fades, *The New York Times*. Retrieved from http://www.nytimes.com/2010/11/19/sports /football/19vick.html?ref=dogfighting

2. Earnheardt, A. (2010). Exploring sports television viewers' judgments of athletes' antisocial behaviors. *International Journal of Sport Communication, 3,* 167–189.

3. Gosling, P., Maxime, D., & Oberle, D. (2006). Denial of responsibility: A new mode of dissonance reduction. *Journal of Personality and Social Psychology, 90*(5), 722–733. doi: 10.1037/0022-3514.90.5.722

12

Lessons Can Be Learned from Athletes' Mistakes

Steve Tobak

Steve Tobak is a management consultant and executive coach with Invisor Consulting. He is a frequent contributor to Inc. *magazine with articles related to career planning and management strategies.*

The cyclist Lance Armstrong doping scandal reveals several traits of superstar athletes that are also common to business executives: fierce competitiveness, a drive to succeed at all costs, and a willingness to put themselves at risk in order to keep pace with the leaders in their field. By taking a close look at the reasons behind Armstrong's willingness to cheat in order to win, we can gain insight into the motivations behind similar scandals in the business world.

There's an age-old saying: "May you live in interesting times."

The enigmatic phrase usually applies to famous or notorious people. Whether it's a blessing or a curse often depends on their actions—such as getting caught doing something they shouldn't have done.

That certainly appears to be the case with Lance Armstrong.

After years of angry denials, the disgraced cyclist finally admitted to doping—to [celebrity host] Oprah Winfrey, no less. He appears to be after some sort of redemption, or at least a diminished ban so he can earn a living racing in triathlons.

The question on everyone's mind is, does he deserve absolution, or did his bad behavior cross a line from which there is no return? To most people, that's a question of ethics and a black-and-white one, at that. Not to me.

While Armstrong's situation may seem unique, it's not.

It's actually quite common in the business world. Many of you may face a similar dilemma at some point in your career, if you haven't already. And like it or not, the path to choose is not as black and white as you might think.

Competitors in All Industries Struggle with Morality

First, let me explain something about Armstrong. He is a fierce competitor who's incredibly focused on winning. That's what drives him. He always has something to prove and a chip on his shoulder about proving it.

Which means he's not unlike some other star athletes, such as former tennis star John McEnroe or Green Bay Packers quarterback Aaron Rodgers. To me, he also sounds a lot like a number of great entrepreneurs and business leaders.

Guys like Donald Trump, George Steinbrenner, Bill Gates, and Larry Ellison come to mind.

A big difference is that Armstrong found himself competing in a sport that has been completely overrun by organized, systematic doping that generates more red blood cells and improves aerobics. If you don't do it, you're at a tremendous disadvantage. And everyone who does it knows exactly how to avoid getting caught.

Once you start down that path, it's a slippery slope.

Not only that, but once you win big and achieve some notoriety that way, it's all too easy to find yourself locked on a treadmill you can't get off. We'll come back to that in a minute.

Now, don't get me wrong. I'm not defending Armstrong's actions. I'm simply suggesting that it's not uncommon to experience similar dilemmas in the business world.

Let me give you a couple of notable examples that come to mind:

Just six years ago, an epidemic of stock option backdating accounting scandals rocked the hightech industry. It took down dozens of top executives from Apple, Altera, Broadcom, Brocade, Cirrus Logic, KLA-Tencor, Maxim, McAfee, Rambus, Sanmini-SCI, Take-Two, Verisign, and Vitesse.

The Apple case tainted the careers of two top executives, former CFO [chief financial officer] Fred D. Anderson and senior VP [vice president] and general counsel Nancy Heinen, both of whom were forever banned from serving as officers or directors of public companies. [Apple chief executive officer (CEO)] Steve Jobs narrowly dodged a bullet because his backdated options had gone underwater, so he had previously had them cancelled and exchanged for restricted shares. That was sheer luck.

Some people are so driven by the need to prove something, by that chip on their shoulder, that they'll do whatever it takes to win. It's a powerful motivation in lots of successful people.

And how about all the top executives that got caught lying on their résumés about degrees they never received? Former chief executive Scott Thompson was shown the door at Yahoo following the Résumé-gate scandal. But Microsemi's board members stood behind CEO James Peterson, even after he lied to them and their shareholders in denying the allegations that later turned out to be true.

Breaking Down Bad Behavior

It's easy to assume that those executives intended malice, but I don't think that's how it typically happens.

I think they embellish their résumés—as many do—when they're young and in desperate need of work. And it follows them throughout their careers. By the time they hit the jackpot and become top executives, it's too late to change their résumés without calling attention to it. There's that treadmill we talked about earlier.

Relating all this back to the Lance Armstrong situation, I think bad behavior often comes down to three major factors:

The age factor. When I was young, I did some stupid things. I know very few people who didn't. Luckily, they didn't amount to much and I didn't get locked into any treadmills I couldn't get off of. I'm incredibly thankful for that. Today, I'm more risk averse because I have so much more to lose, so I'm in little danger of crossing any lines. That clearly wasn't the case with Armstrong and some of the others in the examples above who made bad decisions and perhaps set their paths when they were young.

The denial factor. When it comes to leaders behaving badly, denial is nearly always in play. But any good shrink can tell you that, on some level—probably subconscious—nearly all of us are aware of what we're doing. And if we do bad stuff, it eats at us. So, even if you're good at compartmentalizing bad behavior, a part of your brain feels guilty. And if you are consciously aware of what you're doing, well, who wants to spend their life looking over their shoulder? Not me, that's for sure. It's a lousy way to live. In any case, we all have some capacity for compartmentalization and denial under certain conditions and at certain points in time. All of us.

The ethics factor. Some people are so driven by the need to prove something, by that chip on their shoulder, that they'll do whatever it takes to win. It's a powerful motivation in lots of successful people. And sometimes, they cross a line. For others, ethics and morals are a really big deal. They simply won't cross that line no matter what. I think these two groups of people are at opposing ends of the bell curve, and everyone in the middle has some aspects of both extremes.

So you see, none of this is black and white. That's why I look at Armstrong's redemption in purely practical terms. I'm not interested in what his motivation is for reversing course and coming clean. But if, and only if, he's willing to help expose and bring down the doping culture in cycling, then I think he deserves some leniency and should be allowed to compete in triathlons.

If you're more inclined to be judgmental, that's fine. Let he who is without sin cast the first stone.

13

Sports Scandals Reflect the Culture at Large

Dennis Maley

Dennis Maley is the editor of the Bradenton Times *and a former columnist for* Boxing World *magazine. Prior to his career in journalism, he was a captain in the US Army and participated in the Army World Class Athlete Program as a heavyweight boxer.*

The rash of scandals that have swept professional sports in recent years is not only indicative of widespread corruption in professional athletics; similar corruption has been discovered in the business and political worlds. At the core of these scandals is greed, which is fueled by our culture's infatuation with wealth and material gain. Instead of feigning shock when an athlete fails to live up to society's professed ideals, sports fans should consider how their own values might be contributing to a culture where scandalous behavior is required to get ahead.

Americans seem to love feigning shock any time we are "betrayed" by those we worship, and the media is always willing to sensationalize a story that offers elements of corruption and deceit. But from [cyclist] Lance Armstrong to Major League Baseball, to the crooks on Wall Street who nearly took down the global economy, evidence abounds that we live in a culture of cheating where the rewards for skirting the rules vastly outweigh the punishments for getting caught. It's time to stop blaming the people we enable and take a look at our collective role in creating such an unethical society.

In just the past few years, the sports world has been confronted with the use of performance enhancing drugs more directly than any time in the history of sport. Enough so, that there now seems to be a critical mass of concern in our society, something like a collective shrug asking, *shouldn't we do something here?* Collectively, we don't really seem to have much of an idea of what that should be. It's sort of like gun control. It's obvious something is going terribly wrong in our culture, but where to start?

Both issues face the same primary obstacle—money. Like selling guns, sports is big business and athletes are among the most handsomely-paid members of our society. Just look at Forbes' list of top-paid athletes. Many of them make more than a Fortune 500 CEO [chief executive officer], just through their endorsement deals. Naturally, those who pay the insanely rich athletes are even higher up the food chain. It brings to mind the old [comedian] Chris Rock joke: [Basketball player] Shaquille O'Neal is *rich*; the guy who writes Shaq's checks is *wealthy*. So the stakeholders draw a lot of water, and in a society like ours, where money directly influences influence, change doesn't come easy.

If we stopped paying $200 for "official" replica jerseys, three figures for good seats, $9 for flat, watery beer and $150 for athlete-endorsed $10 shoes made in an Indonesian sweatshop, then the $100 million contracts would dry up quick.

But let's remember *why* top athletes make more than the GDP [gross domestic product] of some small countries. *We* pay them. That's right, stuff all of that nostalgic baloney about how back in the day [baseball players] Lou Gehrig made this or Ted Williams made that. None of them worked for free and none of them ever offered to so far as I know. They earned what the market bore. What *did* happen, was post-WWII prosperity, television, cable and a giant global economy in which international corporations became awash in unthinkable wealth with which to advertise their products.

The value of *everything* went up and when you look at where we dropped our collective dough, sports and entertainment are near the top of the list. So the market for those providing that product exploded and the people most instrumental in delivering it began demanding their fair share. We can gripe about how much it costs to go to an NFL [National Football League] game or get box seats to see the [New York] Yankees, but at the end of the day, it's a market, and the demand sets the value of the supply.

If we stopped paying $200 for "official" replica jerseys, three figures for good seats, $9 for flat, watery beer and $150 for athlete-endorsed $10 shoes made in an Indonesian sweatshop, then the $100 million contracts would dry up quick. *I don't do any of that*, you might say. Well, neither do I, but enough Americans *do* that a market exists. I don't buy Rolls Royces either, but they still sell enough of them to keep the lights on in West Sussex. The same goes for the actor getting $20 million a movie off of the $11 ticket at the multiplex, or the band who's hauling in a fortune on overpriced concert tickets. If an athlete's product is bringing in outrageous sums of money, where should it go? In a capitalist society, why are they any less deserving than the guys who started Facebook?

With such a lofty market out there, it's not only going to draw a lot of aspiring participants, but it's also going to up the ante on what most of them are willing to do to get a ticket on that money train. As consumers, we either reward or punish those decisions, and while a group of sports writers may have kept a bunch of juiced up ball players out of the Hall of Fame, they're still laughing all the way to the bank.

And think about *when* the market for sports exploded the most—during the dawn of the modern PED [performance enhancing drug] era.

Looking for an Edge

To be sure, PED's have been around as long as sport itself. From ancient Greek Olympians using drugs like opium to the gladiators of Rome using stimulants like strychnine, to cocaine's introduction by competitors in various sports in the late 19th century, athletes have always looked for an edge. Most of the time, anything short of rigging a competition by unknowingly sedating someone or paying them to throw the event, was considered fair game. Even during the supposed golden era of baseball, many star players later admitted to using cocaine and other stimulants regularly, which, before steroids, were the premier way to impact performance through drugs.

Nazi Germany experimented with testosterone enhancers as early as the 1930's, but in 1958 things changed for good when Dr. John Bosley Zieglar invented the FDA-approved steroid *Dianabol*, which could effectively synthesize the effects of testosterone, while being easily and cheaply manufactured and administered on a mass scale. This was different than a couple of uppers. Steroids were an ability for athletes to defy DNA, and within 20 years they were commonplace in sports.

Zieglar later denounced his creation when he saw how it was being abused by athletes, but the genie was out of the bottle. Nonetheless, it's useful to remember that the rise of anabolic steroids coincided with advances in sports nutrition, economic factors like abundant and inexpensive meat becoming a much bigger part of the American diet, and scientific applications of weight training. Americans, and athletes in particular, were getting bigger in the 1980's than they had been in previous decades, so the willful suspension of disbelief needed to imagine some of these guys were clean was somewhat mitigated by fans who hadn't grown up in the same era as these young kids. *Maybe it's all this weight training and vitamins they do nowadays?*

As a society, we are quite good at believing the things that confirm our own desires, while ignoring the ever more numerous ones that prove otherwise.

But by the mid-1990's, when all of those things had been a common part of our everyday culture for a generation, it became a bit more difficult to delude ourselves, especially as rapid advancement in PED's (itself driven by the insane money in sports) had greatly changed the degree to which athletes could enhance themselves physically. The ingestion of Human Growth Hormone became more common and better understood scientifically. Existing drugs became more potent and new designer drugs emerged targeting almost every facet of physical performance, drugs that to some extent could circumvent the genetic lottery that had otherwise ruled over professional sports at the highest level.

American sports fans were right there cheering on these new mutant super-athletes. We pretended that it was suddenly possible for men in their late thirties and even 40's to inexplicably add massive amounts of lean muscle mass they didn't have in their teens and 20's, decades after their natural testosterone levels would have peaked; that athletes' hat and sneaker sizes could change in their 20's, long after the human head and feet stop growing; that linebackers who were once considered oversized at 250 lbs. could suddenly weigh up to 300 *and* be faster than running backs of just a generation earlier.

Still, when they get caught doing what everyone knew they were doing in the first place, we say that it is *us* who is disappointed in *them*. I'm sorry, but that seems like blaming a director when you find out the special effects used to blow up the Grand Canyon were CGI [computer generated imagery]. In fact, it also sounds a whole lot like the same self-serving naivete that preceded the run up to financial crises, with everyone from everyday joes to Wall Street CEO's telling themselves (and anyone who'd listen) that the housing bubble could continue to grow infinitely despite basic economic principles, and we could become a nation where everyone was a rich landlord and no one was a humble tenant.

Looking for heroes in the world of professional sports is a fool's errand and it always has been.

Selective Ignorance

As a society, we are quite good at believing the things that confirm our own desires, while ignoring the ever more numerous ones that prove otherwise. Is it a surprise that a nation that found Tony Soprano [main character in the HBO show *The Sopranos*], a homicidal, sociopathic gangster who stole anything within reach, to be its most endearing television character hasn't prosecuted a single banking executive after a global financial crisis supported almost entirely by wholesale fraud? Is it a surprise that a nation reared on superheroes and video games idolizes today's gladiators who by the miracle of modern science have actually been allowed to *look* like the hulking cartoons that once mesmerized us?

In a country where all of the top pop culture—hit music, reality TV, movies, etc.—revolves around tales of gluttonous wealth, wasteful and unsustainable consumption, and other forms of resource-driven debasement; a place where we advertise a legal drug for every possible ailment *plus* a few imagined ones, our *concern* is probably better described as curiosity. Like most things in our culture, we know something is amiss, but then again why wouldn't it be?

What about the example it sets for our children, you might ask? The answer isn't pretty, but in truth, it probably sets an effective example of how to best prosper in such a wicked society—cheat. If you want your children to learn better values, I'd suggest you take care to teach them yourself. Bring them up to find their heroes at home and in their community, and to know that success shouldn't be measured by how many precious resources you can afford to waste air-conditioning a 15,000 square foot home, filling up a fleet of gas-guzzling cars and putting blood diamonds in your watch that some kid in Liberia lost their arm for. Looking for heroes in the world of professional sports is a fool's errand and it always has been. We just used to market athletes differently before the days when the American Dream became keeping up with the Kardashians.

Organizations to Contact

The editors have compiled the following list of organizations concerned with the issues debated in this book. The descriptions are derived from materials provided by the organizations. All have publications or information available for interested readers. The list was compiled on the date of publication of the present volume; names, addresses, phone and fax numbers, and e-mail and Internet addresses may change. Be aware that many organizations take several weeks or longer to respond to inquiries, so allow as much time as possible.

Athletes for a Better World (ABW)
1401 Peachtree St. NE, Suite 500, Atlanta, GA   30309
(404) 892-2328
website: www.abw.org

Athletes for a Better World, founded in 1998, encourages athletes and coaches at all levels to become leaders in society by following an athletic "Code for Living" that emphasizes values learned through participation in sports. The organization offers its "Code for Living" program and resources to athletes, coaches, and parents to help make them better people in all aspects of life. ABW supports numerous awards and scholarships for student athletes, and its website includes stories about past recipients as well as other resources.

Athletes for Charity
United Charitable Programs, 6201 Leesburg Pike, Suite 405
Falls Church, VA   22044
(703) 536-8708
e-mail: info@athletesforcharity.com
website: www.athletesforcharity.com

Athletes for Charity, an affiliate of United Charitable Programs, partners with a number of individual athletes and charities founded by athletes to support programs helping underprivileged children, including foster care and public education.

Major League Baseball (MLB)
Office of the Commissioner of Baseball
Allan H. (Bud) Selig, Commissioner, 245 Park Ave., 31st Floor
New York, NY   10167
(212) 931-7800 • fax: (212) 949-5654
website: www.mlb.com

Major League Baseball is the highest-level league in baseball, consisting of thirty teams (twenty-nine in the United States and one in Canada). It regulates the sport, negotiates labor agreements, handles marketing and media contracts, determines punishments for players that violate codes of conduct, and hires umpires.

Major League Baseball Players Association (MLBPA)
12 East 49th St., 24th Floor, New York, NY   10017
(212) 826-0808 • fax: (212) 752-4378
e-mail: feedback@mlbpa.org
website: http://mlb.mlb.com/pa/index.jsp

The Major League Baseball Players Association, founded in 1953, is the union of all Major League Baseball (MLB) players. It represents these players in collective bargaining with MLB, challenges punishments handed down by the league, and serves as the players' group licensing agent.

National Basketball Association (NBA)
Attn: Fan Relations, 645 Fifth Ave., New York, NY   10022
(212) 407-8000 • fax: (212) 832-3861
website: www.nba.com

The National Basketball Association is the highest-level professional basketball league in North America. It is made up of thirty teams (twenty-nine in the United States and one in Canada). Among its responsibilities are regulating the rules of the game and athlete conduct, marketing the sport, and negotiating labor contracts with the players' association (the NBPA).

National Basketball Players Association (NBPA)

310 Lenox Ave., New York, NY   10027
(212) 655-0880 • fax: (212) 655-0881
e-mail: info@nbpa.com
website: www.nbpa.org/

The National Basketball Players Association, formed in 1954, is the union for all players in the National Basketball Association (NBA). It represents the players in collective bargaining agreements with the NBA and provides players with other types of support, including assistance with filing grievances and rehabilitation after scandal.

National Football League (NFL)

345 Park Ave., New York, NY   10017
website: www.nfl.com

The National Football League, the highest-level American football league, consists of thirty-two teams. It regulates the rules of the game and player conduct, negotiates labor agreements with the players' union (the NFLPA), and promotes the game of football in the United States and around the world.

National Football League Players Association (NFLPA)

1133 20th St. NW, Washington, DC   20036
(202) 756-9100 • fax: (202) 756-9320
website: www.nflplayers.com

The National Football League Players Association (NFLPA) is the union representing all players in the National Football League (NFL). It was founded in 1956. It provides support for players in challenging punishments and fines, negotiates labor agreements through collective bargaining with the NFL, and provides various other types of support to its members.

National Hockey League (NHL)

1185 Avenue of the Americas, 12th Floor
New York, NY   10036

(212) 789-2000 • fax: (212) 789-2020
website: www.nhl.com

The National Hockey League, one of the four major professional sports leagues in North America, governs professional ice hockey and its players. It consists of thirty teams in the United States and Canada.

National Hockey League Players' Association (NHLPA)
20 Bay St., Suite 1700, Toronto, ON
  M5J 2N8
website: www.nhlpa.com

The National Hockey League Players' Association, founded in 1967, is the union representing all players in the National Hockey League (NHL). It engages in labor negotiations with the NHL and assists players with public relations, marketing, and licensing.

Public Relations Society of America (PRSA)
33 Maiden Lane, 11th Floor, New York, NY   10038-5150
(212) 460-1400
e-mail: research@prsa.org
website: www.prsa.org

The Public Relations Society of America is a national association of public relations (PR) professionals. Athletes frequently hire PR firms to help restore their reputation after a scandal.

Special Olympics
1133 19th St. NW, Washington, DC   20036-3604
(202) 628-3630
e-mail: info@specialolympics.org
website: www.specialolympics.org/

The goal of the Special Olympics is to provide sports training and athletic competition in a variety of Olympic-type sports for children and adults with intellectual disabilities, thereby giving them continuing opportunities to develop physical fitness and to experience the joy of participating in sport. The organization's website offers information on the various sporting events sponsored by the Special Olympics and news about athletes and recent competitions.

Women's National Basketball Association (WNBA)

Attn: Fan Services, 645 Fifth Ave., New York, NY 10022
(212) 688-9622 • fax: (212) 750-9622
website: www.wnba.com

The Women's National Basketball Association, founded in 1996, consists of twelve teams in the United States. It oversees league operations and player conduct, engages in labor negotiations with the players' association (the WNBPA), and negotiates marketing and broadcasting agreements. Most WNBA teams share an arena with a men's league (NBA) counterpart.

Women's National Basketball Players Association (WNBPA)

310 Lenox Ave., New York, NY 10027
(212) 655-0880 • fax: (212) 655-0881
e-mail: info@nbpa.com
website: www.wnbpa.org

The Women's National Basketball Players Association represents players in the Women's National Basketball Association (WNBA). Formed in 1998, it was the first labor union in women's professional sports.

Bibliography

Books

Steve Bailey   *Athlete First: A History of the
                      Paralympic Movement.* Chichester,
                      United Kingdom: John Wiley & Sons,
                      2008.

Joel Best   *Everyone's a Winner: Life in Our
                      Congratulatory Culture.* Berkeley, CA:
                      University of California Press, 2011.

Tom Bunevich   *Sign This: The Real Truth About Your
                      Sports Heroes and the Sports
                      Autograph Industry.* Tampa, FL: T&S
                      Publishing, 2000.

David M. Carter   *On the Ball: What You Can Learn
and Darren   About Business from America's Sports
Rovell   Leaders.* Upper Saddle River, NJ:
                      Prentice Hall/Financial Times, 2003.

Fred Coalter   *A Wider Social Role for Sport: Who's
                      Keeping the Score?* London, United
                      Kingdom: Routledge, 2007.

Simon C. Darnell   *Sport for Development and Peace: A
                      Critical Sociology.* London, United
                      Kingdom: Bloomsbury Academic,
                      2012.

Debbie Elicksen   *Positive Sports: Professional Athletes
                      and Mentoring Youth.* Calgary,
                      Canada: Freelance Communications,
                      2003.

Randolph M. Feezell	*Sport, Philosophy, and Good Lives.* Lincoln, NE: University of Nebraska Press, 2013.
John Garrity	*Real Sports Heroes: Athletes Who Made a Difference.* Kingston, NY: Total Sports Publishing, 2001.
John M. Hoberman	*Darwin's Athletes: How Sport Has Damaged Black America and Preserved the Myth of Race.* Boston, MA: Houghton Mifflin, 1997.
Kathryn Jay	*More than Just a Game: Sports in American Life Since 1945.* New York: Columbia University Press, 2004.
M.J. McNamee	*Sports, Virtues and Vices: Morality Plays.* London, United Kingdom: Routledge, 2008.
Patrick B. Miller and David K. Wiggins	*Sport and the Color Line: Black Athletes and Race Relations in Twentieth-Century America.* New York: Routledge, 2004.
Geoff Nichols	*Sport and Crime Reduction: The Role of Sports in Tackling Youth Crime.* London, United Kingdom: Routledge, 2007.
Michael Novak	*The Joy of Sports: End Zones, Bases, Baskets, Balls, and the Consecration of the American Spirit,* rev. ed. Lanham, MD: Madison Books, 1994.
David C. Ogden and Joel Nathan Rosen, eds.	*Fame to Infamy: Race, Sport, and the Fall from Grace.* Jackson, MS: University Press of Mississippi, 2010.

Thomas O'Toole   *Champions of Faith: Catholic Sports Heroes Tell Their Stories.* Franklin, WI: Sheed & Ward, 2001.

Sandra S. Prettyman   *Learning Culture Through Sports: Exploring the Role of Sports in Society.* Lanham, MD: Rowman & Littlefield, 2006.

Ken Rappoport and Barry Wilner   *They Changed the Game: Sports Pioneers of the Twentieth Century.* Kansas City, MO: Andrews McMeel Publishing, 1999.

Stanley H. Teitelbaum   *Sports Heroes, Fallen Idols.* Lincoln, NE: University of Nebraska Press, 2008.

Deborah V. Tudor   *Hollywood's Vision of Team Sports: Heroes, Race, and Gender.* New York: Garland, 1997.

Lawrence A. Wenner, ed.   *Fallen Sports Heroes, Media, and Celebrity Culture.* New York: P. Lang, 2013.

Janet Woolum   *Outstanding Women Athletes: Who They Are and How They Influenced Sports in America.* Phoenix, AZ: Oryx Press, 1992.

Periodicals and Internet Sources

José M. Alamillo "Beyond the Latino Sports Hero: The Role of Sports in Creating Communities, Networks, and Identities," National Park Service, n.d. (accessed April 5, 2013). www .nps.gov.

Steve Buckley and Karen Guregian "Boston's Sports Stars Take the Lead: Athletes Recognize, Embrace Their Duty in Helping City Heal from Marathon Bombings," *Boston Herald*, April 28, 2013. http://bostonherald .com.

Mac Engel "Commentary: A True Hero Remembered in the Home of Sports 'Heroes,'" *McClatchy DC*, February 16, 2013. www.mcclatchydc.com.

Bob Frantz "Today's Sports Stars Fail to Set a Good Example for Young Athletes," *SF Examiner*, August 14, 2011. www.sfexaminer.com.

Simon Kuper "Dangerous Myth of the Role Model Athlete," *Financial Times*, February 15, 2013. www.ft.com.

Andrew Skinner Lopata "Athletes Can Set Example on Domestic Violence," *Eugene (OR) Register-Guard*, March 3, 2010. http://special.registerguard.com.

Miranda Murphy "Sports Heroes Are Needed," *Southeast Sun*, March 14, 2013. www.southeastsun.com.

William S. Paxton "Musial Last of Our Sports Heroes,"
Connecticut Post, January 27, 2013.
www.ctpost.com.

Leonard Pitts Jr. "Gay Athletes Need to Be True Sports
Heroes," *Detroit Free Press*, March 8,
2013. www.freep.com.

Bill Zuck "Use Sports Role Models the Right
Way," *Sun Chronicle*, February 10,
2013. www.thesunchronicle.com.

Index

A

Abdul-Jabbar, Kareem, 29–30, 32
African American athletes
  black athletic boogeyman
    concept, 31–32
  must speak out, 32–33
  overview, 29–31
  role models, right and duty,
    29–33
Ahrens, Christopher, 55–60
Aikman, Troy, 14
Alcindor, Lew, 29
Ali, Muhammad, 30, 32
Amateur Athletic Union, 25
American Football Conference
  (AFC), 52
Anabolic steroids, 78
Ancient Greek athletes, 7, 50–51
Anderson, Fred D., 72
Armstrong, Lance
  doping confession, 9, 11, 16–
    17, 24, 70–71
  loss of endorsements, 26, 62
Arthurian legend, 20
A.T. Kearny (consulting), 7
Athlete scandals
  breaking down bad behavior,
    73–74
  endorsements and, 61–62
  fans opinions of, 65–69
  fan support and, 66–68
  lessons learned from, 70–74
  looking for and edge, 78–80
  moral clauses and, 61–64
  morality in all industries,
    71–72

  new kinds of, 63–64
  overview, 61–63, 65–66, 70–71
  reflection of culture, 75–81
  selective ignorance over,
    80–81
  as sensational, 75–78
Athletes as role models
  can help end homophobia,
    40–43
  cost of great achievement,
    21–22
  female athlete role models,
    34–39
  giving back, 13–15
  influence on society, 11–15
  inner drive, 19–21
  inner worth of, 17–19
  introduction, 7–10
  overview, 11–13, 16–17
  in physical education, 56–57
  unfair to expect, 16–22
  See also Christian athletes;
    Sports heroes
Ayanbadejo, Brendon, 40–43

B

Banned substance use, 9, 52, 64
Barkley, Charles, 8, 12, 23–24, 28,
  50
Benirschke, Rolf, 14
Berlin Olympics (1936), 25
Bin Laden, Osama, 31, 62
Black athletic boogeyman concept,
  31–32
Bonds, Barry, 9, 24, 31
Bradley, Bill, 27
Brooklyn Dodgers, 41

Brown, Jim, 29, 32
Bryant, Kobe, 9, 26

C

Carlos, John, 30
Carnera, Primo, 24
Carter, Leeja, 65–69
Castro, Ivan, 59
Chase, Christopher R., 61–64
Child sexual-abuse scandal, 26–27
Christian athletes
    in action, 50–53
    new era of, 47–48
    not role models, 49–54
    overview, 44–46
    as role models, 44–48
    signs of grace and, 53–54
Clemens, Roger, 9, 24
Cold War, 8
Collective bargaining agreement
    (CBA), 13
Collins, Jason, 10, 40–41
Collins, Kerry, 14
Copeland, Kenneth, 46
Cowherd, Colin, 30–31
Crescent Moon Foundation, 14
Cribb, Bryan, 44–48

D

Daytona 500, 35
Deford, Frank, 52
Denial factor in bad behavior, 73
Dianabol (steroid), 78
Disabled veterans as role models,
    57–59

E

Ellison, Larry, 71
Ethics factor in bad behavior,
    73–74
Evans, Lee, 30

F

Federal Bureau of Investigation
    (FBI), 25
Female athlete role models
    broader horizons, 36–39
    empower young women,
      34–39
    overview, 34–36
Forever Young Foundation, 14

G

Galli, Mark, 49–54
Galloway, Noah, 58–59
Gates, Bill, 71
Gehrig, Lou, 76
Goodell, Roger, 31

H

Harrison, James, 31
Heinen, Nancy, 72
Hernandez, Aaron, 52
Heroes, Saviors, Traitors, and Su-
    permen: A History of Hero Wor-
    ship (Hughes-Hallett), 27
Hill, Grant, 32
Holy Grail legend, 20
Homophobia
    athletes help end, 40–43
    coming out, 42–43
    overview, 40–42

Hughes-Hallett, Lucy, 27–28
Human Growth Hormone, 79

J

James, Edgerrin, 14
Jobs, Steve, 72
Jones, Marion, 9
Jordan, Michael, 8, 17–19, 21, 22

K

Kaepernick, Colin, 50, 52–53
Kansas City Royals, 36
Karros, Eric, 14
Kicks For Critters, 14
King, Billie Jean, 8
Kruk, John, 49–50

L

Lakeshore Foundation, 58
Leon, Carlos, 57–58
Lesbian, gay, bisexual, and trans-
gender (LGBT) Americans, 42
Lewis, Lennox, 14
Lewis, Ray, 50, 52
Lima Foxtrot Programs for In-
jured Military, 58
Lin, Jeremy, 44–48
Livestrong, 26
Los Angeles Lakers, 9
Los Angeles Times (newspaper), 24
Louis, Joe, 24–25

M

Major League Baseball, 40
Maley, Dennis, 75–81
Malone, Karl, 8–9

Mastro, James, 55–60
McEnroe, John, 71
McGwire, Mark, 9
Mendenhall, Rashard, 31, 62–63
Moon, Warren, 14
Moral clauses for athletes, 61–64

N

National Association for Stock Car
Auto Racing (NASCAR), 35
National Basketball Association
(NBA), 8, 12, 31, 40, 44
National Collegiate Athletic Asso-
ciation (NCAA) College Basket-
ball Tournament, 7
National Football League (NFL),
36, 41–42, 46, 77
National Hockey League (NHL),
41
National Wheelchair Athletic As-
sociation, 56
New York Knicks, 44
New York Post (newspaper), 25
Nike, 24, 26, 61

O

Obama, Barack, 42
Olsen, Jack, 29–30
The Olympics, 7
O'Neal, Shaquille, 76
Owens, Jesse, 24–25

P

Paralympians
disabled veterans as role models, 57–59
as inspirational, 55–60

overview, 55–56
role models in physical education, 56–57
summary, 59–60
Paralympic Military Sports Program, 58
Para-Panamerican Games, 57
Parents as role models, 8, 12
Parsley, Rod, 46
Paterno, Joe, 26–27
Patrick, Danica, 10, 34–39
Performance enhancing drugs (PEDs), 9, 78–79
Petersen, James, 72
Piper, John, 45
Pistorius, Oscar, 17, 20
Pittsburgh Steelers, 9
Posnanski, Joe, 34–39
Professional Golfers' Association (PGA), 36

R

Reese, Pee Wee, 41, 43
Religion News Service, 45
Rhoden, William C., 23–28
Riggs, Bobby, 8
Robeson, Paul, 25
Robinson, Jackie, 8, 40–41
Rock, Chris, 76
Rodgers, Aaron, 71
Rodriguez, Alex, 65
Roethlisberger, Ben, 9
Russell, Bill, 29

S

Sandusky, Jerry, 26–27
Seau, Junior, 11–12
Seinfeld, Jerry, 36–37

Sexual assault accusations, 9
Smith, Andre, 11
Smith, Tommie, 30
Social-media activities, 64
Sosa, Sammy, 9
Soviet Union, 8
Sports heroes (heroism)
emotion of, 24–25
hypocrisy of, 25–26
illusion of, 23–28
overview, 23–24
tragedy of, 26–28
Sports Illustrated (magazine), 8, 31, 52
Stanley Cup playoffs, 7
Statton, Nathan, 55–60
Steenkamp, Reeva, 17, 20
Steinberg, Leigh, 11–15
Steinbrenner, George, 71
Stenhouse, Ricky, Jr., 36
Strug, Kerri, 8
Super Bowl, 7, 50

T

Tebow, Tim, 46–48, 51
Te'o, Manti, 11
Third and Long program, 14
Thomas, Derrick, 14
Thomas, Etan, 31
Thompson, Scott, 72
Thompson, Wright, 17–19
Tillery, Mike, 29–33
Tobak, Steve, 70–74
Tour de France, 9, 11, 16
Trinity Broadcasting Network, 46
Trump, Donald, 71
Tyson, Mike, 17

U

United States Anti-Doping Agency, 63

United States Association of Blind Athletes (USABA), 56

US men's ice hockey team, 8

US women's gymnastics team, 8

V

Values of the Game (Bradley), 27

Veterans Performance Program, 57–58

Vick, Michael, 9, 24, 62, 65, 68

W

Wallace, Lane, 16–22

Walter Reed Army Medical Center, 58

Williams, Deron, 32

Williams, Ted, 77

Winfrey, Oprah, 11, 70

Woods, Tiger, 9, 24, 26, 62, 65, 68

World Cup, 7

World Series, 7

Y

Young, Steve, 14

Z

Zieglar, John Bosley, 78